CHRISTIANITY'S FAMILY TREE

Other Books by Adam Hamilton

Confronting the Controversies
Leading Beyond the Walls
Unleashing the Word
Making Love Last a Lifetime
Christianity and World Religions
Selling Swimsuits in the Arctic

Video Studies by Adam Hamilton

Making Love Last a Lifetime
Confronting the Controversies
Christianity and World Religions

For more information, please go to www.abingdonpress.com

ADAM HAMILTON

CHRISTIANITY'S FAMILY TREE

WHAT OTHER CHRISTIANS BELIEVE AND WHY

ABINGDON PRESS

NASHVILLE

CHRISTIANITY'S FAMILY TREE:
WHAT OTHER CHRISTIANS BELIEVE AND WHY

Copyright © 2007 by Abingdon Press.

This book is printed on acid-free, elemental chlorine-free paper.

ISBN 978-0-687-49116-2

14 15 16 17—15 14 13 12
MANUFACTURED IN THE UNITED STATES OF AMERICA

To my friends Jeff Adams, Vernon Armitage,
Paul Brooks, Doug Rumford, and George Westlake.

From Sojourners website (by Stephen Mattson)

A misconception that the Bible is the ultimate answer book & Christianity a divine encyclopedia presenting the solutions to life's biggest Q. The Xian faith is about a relationship w/ Christ instead of an academic collection of right/wrong doctrines. Focus on getting to know Jesus. Never let a desire for being right obstruct your love for Christ.

Xianity is complex & diverse — ask more Q to learn. Be OK w/not knowing.

Living a life like Jesus is not safe, logical, or a way to avoid the harsh realities of life.

Instead of theology & theory, our faith sh be full of practice, action & interaction. Admit struggles, sins, discomfort, vulnerability. Xian community is messy, hard work. Embrace this reality. God is perfect. Christianity is not. Focus less on growth, power, influence, popularity, fame, # or stats; instead, follow Jesus' example to the best of our ability: love everyone, serve the poor, feed the hungry, tend the sick, forgive our enemies, accept the outcast, embrace the needy, give sacrificially.

Xianity is about introducing others to God, & growing closer to God.

ACKNOWLEDGMENTS

This book would not be possible without the support of the congregation I serve as senior pastor, the United Methodist Church of the Resurrection. This book was first a sermon series during which, for eight weeks in a row, we changed our worship style each week to reflect the worship patterns of the various denominations and traditions we were studying. Many congregations would have chafed under the weekly disruption of their own worship traditions, but our members were energized by it. The end result of this series of sermons was that I felt our congregation members had grown in their faith and in their appreciation of other Christians. It was this result that led me to believe others would benefit from a book based upon these sermons.

I am grateful for the staff and pastors at the Church of the Resurrection who helped in implementing the sermons and whose ideas and thoughts helped shape my own thoughts in ways too numerous to mention. I am humbled and honored to serve Christ with such a remarkable group. I want specifically to mention Sue Thompson, my assistant, whose research and work in setting up interviews with each of the denominational

7

leaders I interviewed for this study were invaluable. I would also mention Connie Stella and Kristin Thompson, whose work made possible the video interviews in the small-group resource that can be used alongside this book.

I am indebted to each of the denominational leaders I met with and interviewed for this book: Father Timothy Sawchak of the Russian Orthodox Church, Dr. Claude Sasso of the Roman Catholic Church, Bishop Gerald Mansholt of the Evangelical Lutheran Church of America, Dr. Doug Rumford and Dr. Tom Are of the Presbyterian Church of America, the Very Reverend Terry White of the Episcopal Church, Dr. Jeff Adams of the Independent Baptist Church, Dr. George Westlake of the Assembly of God Church, and Bishop Scott Jones of The United Methodist Church.

Thanks also to Dr. Bill J. Leonard, dean and professor of church history at Wake Forest University Divinity School, for reading the manuscript and making suggestions.

Finally, my special thanks to Rob Simbeck, whose help in editorial revisions and transforming my sermon manuscripts into book chapters was invaluable.

CONTENTS

A FAMILY REUNION

Imagine yourself walking into a big family reunion. People stand around the room in little groups, talking and laughing. Some are beginning to line up at a long table filled with an incredible array of homemade food. They fill their plates, walk to tables, and begin dining. As you look around, you see folks you simply do not recognize. There are others that you recognize but are unable to place with certainty on the family tree and still others who prompt you to think, *Are you sure I'm related to* them? Inevitably, some of those in attendance will be quite a bit different from you. Your natural inclination as you fill your plate might be to sit with folks you already know and see with some regularity, to avoid talking with those you seldom see.

My mother's side of the family had a reunion not long ago; and I found that when it came time to eat, I wanted to sit next to my brothers and sisters. I was finding it difficult to remember who all these other people were and what my relationship with them was—which ones were second cousins three times removed and which were third cousins only twice removed! At some point in the afternoon, though, I came to a realization.

I had a great-grandmother we used to visit as kids. I have many fond memories of going to her home. And here was my realization: She was the mother, grandmother, great-grandmother, or great-great-grandmother of every single person in that room. She was how we were connected! Consequently I found myself listening more intently as I made my way around the room. I was getting to know my family; and as I listened to their stories, I was learning something about myself.

In this book we will study our family in the faith. Going through its pages will be a lot like attending a family reunion. We will be getting to know some strange cousins in whose presence we might initially feel a bit uncomfortable. We will wonder what our connection is to these folks. In the end, though, as we look at the various branches of Christianity, we will come to see that we share one Father, one Lord and Savior, and one Holy Spirit—we are family. And if we take the time to listen to our family, we will come to know God, and ourselves, a bit better.

In this book we will learn about church history, theology, and Christian spirituality, seeing what it is that makes each branch of our Christian family unique. The aim of this book is not to critique the various churches and traditions we will study. Neither is it to compare and contrast them. Instead my aim is to help you learn from your brothers and sisters of other denominations so that your faith might be enriched and that we might be more authentic and effective disciples of Jesus Christ.

Please keep in mind that this is not an academic study, and I am not a church historian. I am a pastor, seeking to introduce people to a subject about which I care passionately. As a result, my descriptions of the various Christian denominations and faith traditions may not be as accurate or complete as those you would encounter in a seminary class or textbook. Rather than comprehensiveness, my aim has been to capture something of the unique personality of each of these groups, engaging your imagination and inspiring you, I would hope, to further reading on your own. To that end, I have included a list of books you can read for follow-up study, along with a brief description of each.

You might want to know a little more about my place in this family of faith, since I will be walking with you through this reunion. I am a member of the United Methodist Church, and I will readily admit that it is the Methodists I would be most tempted to sit with in our imaginary reunion. But I am very close to the Catholics as well. My father and his family were Roman Catholic; my mother was from a conservative Protestant background. I was baptized a Catholic. My Catholic grandmother was among the most-pivotal spiritual influences of my early childhood. My first Bible was one she gave our family. She taught me to pray the Our Father and the Rosary, and she took me to Mass whenever she could. My faith was also shaped by my mother and her conservative Christian faith which shared many characteristics with the Baptist traditions. My godfather is a leader in the Greek Orthodox Church. I came to a personal faith in Christ in a Pentecostal church. And in college, after reading the stories of John Wesley, I became a United Methodist. At college my daughter occasionally worships in an Episcopal church. And I have several good friends who are Presbyterians.

My point is that each of these traditions we will study together has shaped my life and faith. I have worshiped in each of the churches described in this book and have learned and grown from my exposure to each of them. All of which is to say that I am personally indebted to several different faith traditions, and it is out of that appreciation for these other Christians that I write this book.

You will see that I have presented the various Christian traditions in roughly the order in which they developed, to help readers trace the growth of the Christian family tree. One exception is the chapter on Methodism, which, as a United Methodist pastor, I have chosen to present last, even though it is not the newest of the traditions.

Having said that, however, I want to be clear that the focus in this book is not to convince you that United Methodists are better Christians than others. I am hoping that all of us, of whatever denomination, can learn from one another and, by listening to others, can become more-faithful Christians. My aim in each of these chapters is to help us learn from the traditions we are studying and to allow each of them to deepen our own faith and our experience of God.

Walk with me, then, through this reunion of our most-extraordinary and interesting family.

CHAPTER 1

ORTHODOXY: MYSTERY, LITURGY, AND TRADITION

*Now faith is the assurance of things hoped for, the convic-
tion of things not seen. Indeed, by faith our ancestors received
approval. By faith we understand that the worlds were prepared by the word of God, so that what is seen was made from
things that are not visible. . . .*

*By faith Abraham obeyed when he was called to set out for
a place that he was to receive as an inheritance; and he set out,
not knowing where he was going. By faith he stayed for a time
in the land he had been promised, as in a foreign land, living
in tents, as did Isaac and Jacob, who were heirs with him of the
same promise. For he looked forward to the city that has foundations, whose architect and builder is God. . . .*

*All of these died in faith without having received the prom-
ises, but from a distance they saw and greeted them. They con-
fessed that they were strangers and foreigners on the earth, for
people who speak in this way make it clear that they are seeking a homeland. If they had been thinking of the land that they
had left behind, they would have had opportunity to return. But
as it is, they desire a better country, that is, a heavenly one.
Therefore God is not ashamed to be called their God; indeed,
he has prepared a city for them.*

Therefore, since we are surrounded by so great a cloud of witnesses, let us also lay aside every weight and the sin that clings so closely, and let us run with perseverance the race that is set before us, looking to Jesus the pioneer and perfecter of our faith, who for the sake of the joy that was set before him endured the cross, disregarding its shame, and has taken his seat at the right hand of the throne of God.
(Hebrews 11:1-3, 8-10, 13-16; 12:1-2)

In the Beginning:
From Jesus to Christianity to Orthodoxy

We will begin the study of our Christian family by looking at the church that claims to be the oldest child: the Orthodox church. But first we will want to gain a little perspective by tracing some of our ancient family tree.

Christianity, of course, began within Judaism, making the Jews an important part of our family. Our Scriptures, worship patterns, and organizational structure were in large part shaped by Judaism. Then, as Christianity began to develop and incorporate more and more non-Jews, it became increasingly distinct from Judaism. At this stage, in the first centuries of the Christian faith, Jesus' followers were not Orthodox or Roman Catholic. They were known as Nazarenes, or followers of Jesus of Nazareth; as followers of "the Way"; or simply as "Christians," followers of Jesus Christ.

In the ensuing centuries, arguments over theology and practice led to great conflict within the church, whose leaders called together bishops from throughout the world to hash out the essentials of the faith we share. That meeting took place in AD 325 in the city of Nicaea, and the resulting statement of faith is called the Nicene Creed. (The creed as we know it today includes significant additions made at a subsequent council in 381 at Constantinople, and for this reason it is occasionally called the Nicene-Constantinopolitan Creed.) Despite this unity of belief, there were great differences between Christians in the eastern and western halves of the Roman Empire. These differences, more cultural, philosophical, and political than theological, were in fact tearing the empire apart.

Emperor Constantine, who had reunited the empire, appointed his sons to rule after his death. One, ruling from the traditional capital of Rome, was trying to ward off the continuing invasions of barbarians; the other ruled in the Greek-speaking East from the capital city of Constantinople, considered the new Rome.

Christians in the Latin-speaking West tended to see the gospel in concrete terms, with the juridical models of sin and justice as keys to its understanding. Those in the East made greater allowance for mystery, for experiencing God, and for an understanding of salvation rooted in our experience of death and resurrection.

Through the centuries, as contact between the halves of the old empire lessened, the gulf between East and West widened. Questions about the relationship of the four major leaders of the Christian churches in the East (known as patriarchs) with the prince among leaders in the Western church (the pope) were particularly thorny. While the patriarchs recognized the pope's status as first among equals, they did not believe he had authority over their churches.

Then, in the seventh century, at a regional council in Toledo, Spain, Western Christians added three little words to the Nicene Creed without consulting Eastern Christians. These three little words, called the "filioque" (Latin for "from the Son"), stated that the Holy Spirit proceeded not only from the Father, which everyone agreed upon, but also from the Son. The Eastern Christians expressed their dismay with the Western Christians. Conflicts over papal authority, liturgy, and the ever-present filioque continued for centuries; and then in 1054, Pope Leo X (actually his legate) and Patriarch Michael I excommunicated each other and all the other's followers from the church, creating a breach that has lasted until the present.

Each church we will study sees church history in a slightly different way. Orthodox Christians believe they are the direct and continuous successors of the apostles and that the Roman Catholic Church, by adding to the creed, giving too much authority to the pope, and changing liturgy, departed from the right path. The following illustration depicts how Orthodoxy views itself as well as Roman Catholicism and Protestantism:

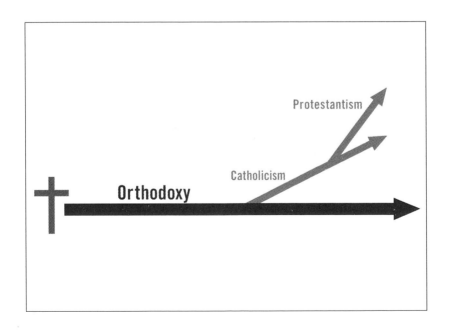

The Eastern Christians claimed the title "Orthodox," a word that means "right worship" and "right doctrine." The name makes a strong statement. Eastern Christians, by virtue of this name, claim to have the right forms of worship and doctrine while, by implication, Western Christians do not. If Eastern Christians are the Orthodox church, then all other Christians are *not* Orthodox. In other words, one might say that we, the 2.1 billion other Christians in the world, are heretics. It is important to know that this is the official stance of the Orthodox church, that they are the one true church. When it comes to the possibility of salvation for the rest of us, the Orthodox clergy I have read and spoken to are a bit agnostic—What God chooses to do with non-Orthodox followers of Jesus at Judgment Day is up to God—but they are unapologetic when it comes to the assertion that they are the true church.

Today, Eastern Orthodox Christianity makes up the second-largest body of Christians after Roman Catholics. Its members continue to be located largely in the East, with the single largest number of Orthodox Christians being found in Russia. Within Eastern Orthodoxy the divisions are largely ethnic. There are Russian Orthodox, Greek Orthodox, Syrian Orthodox, and a host of others; but they all are part of the one Orthodox church. It is difficult to ascertain the total number of practicing Orthodox "adherents," and estimates range from 95 million to as many as 300 million.

We begin with this particular church in part because it claims to preserve the earliest traditions of the Christian faith and in part because it is associated with the earliest centers of Christianity, namely, Jerusalem and Antioch.

Orthodox Beliefs and Practices

The Nicene Creed

"We are the church of the apostles," says Orthodox priest Father Timothy Sawchak of the Holy Trinity Orthodox Church in Overland Park, Kansas. He cites Pentecost as "the beginning of our church" and says, "We base our doctrine initially on Christ and Scriptures—the Old and New Testaments—and also on the ecumenical councils that were able to put down in words what we believe." Those beliefs are summarized in the Nicene Creed, which is recited at each celebration of the liturgy:

We believe in one God, the Father, the Almighty, maker of heaven and earth, of all that is, seen and unseen.

We believe in one Lord, Jesus Christ, the only Son of God, eternally begotten of the Father, God from God, Light from Light, true God from true God, begotten, not made, of one Being with the Father, through him all things were made. For us and for our salvation he came down from heaven; by the power of the Holy Spirit he became incarnate from the Virgin Mary, and became truly human. For our sake he was crucified under Pontius Pilate; he suffered death and was buried.

On the third day he rose again in accordance with the Scriptures; he ascended into heaven and is seated at the right hand of the Father. He will come again in glory to judge the living and the dead, and his kingdom will have no end.

We believe in the Holy Spirit, the Lord, the giver of life, who proceeds from the Father. Who with the Father is worshiped and glorified, who has spoken through the Prophets. We believe in one holy catholic and apostolic Church. We acknowledge one baptism for the forgiveness of sins. We look for the resurrection of the dead, and the life of the world to come. Amen.[1]

What I want you to notice is that this is the prince of creeds in the Roman Catholic and mainline Protestant church as well, with the exception of the statement on the Holy Spirit, where Roman Catholics and Protestants follow the Western addition of the three words indicating that the Holy Spirit proceeds from the Father and the Son. Otherwise, in these essentials of the faith, the majority of Christians are in agreement.

The Human Condition, Salvation, and Sanctification

In addition to the controversy over the filioque, there are other differences that developed between Eastern and Western Christianity. Orthodox teaching regarding the human condition is not tied to the doctrine of original sin, that Adam and Eve's sin is now passed on to all humankind. What is passed on from Adam and Eve is death and all that death brings: anger, lust, hate, greed, fear, sickness. As a result of Adam and Eve's sin, humanity was placed in the grip of death and the devil. We are slaves to death. Jesus came to give his life as a ransom for all humanity, to redeem humankind from death and the devil by giving his own life. He set us free. Human beings, once this gift is accepted, begin a lifelong journey toward becoming like God.[2]

The aim of the Christian life is this goal of becoming like God, of being transformed and made holy, of becoming a new creation. In some traditions this is referred to as sanctification. Among the means of accomplishing this transformation are participation in worship—the Divine Liturgy—as well as prayer and pursuit of the seven mysteries or sacraments. Like Roman Catholics, the Orthodox recognize seven official sacraments, while maintaining that a host of things may function as sacraments (means of God's grace coming into our lives). The Orthodox believe that each of the sacraments is used by the Holy Spirit to impart grace and make us holy. The Christian life begins at baptism; and until one is baptized, one is outside the church. Baptism in Orthodox churches is by immersion, and even infants are immersed completely under the water. Anointing with oil (chrismation) follows immediately after baptism. This takes the place of confirmation, so that one is fully a member of the church at baptism. Among the first acts after baptism is the reception of the Eucharist; a drop of wine is placed on the tongue of the infant.

The priest who baptizes and offers the Eucharist will be a man; women are not ordained in the Orthodox church. Unlike the Roman Catholic Church, priests may marry, provided they have married before ordination.

Scripture and Tradition

An important part of understanding Orthodoxy is understanding the role of the Fathers of the church in shaping Christian doctrine and practice.

"The fundamental witness to the Christian tradition," says Father Michael Azkoul of the Orthodox church, "is Holy Scripture; and the supreme expositors of the Scriptures are the divinely inspired Fathers of the church, whether the Greek Fathers or Latin Fathers, Syriac Fathers or Slavic Fathers. Their place in the Orthodox religion cannot be challenged. Their authority cannot be superseded, altered, or ignored."[3]

This is important. Sometimes Protestant Christians look at the Bible and believe that not much happened between the time of the apostles and the time of the Protestant Reformation. But the Orthodox believe that the Holy Spirit was guiding the early church and that, therefore, the Christians of the first five centuries were important interpreters of the Scriptures. The writings of these Christians function for the Orthodox in some ways like the Mishnah and the Talmud (scriptural interpretations and commentaries) function in Judaism. The Protestant idea of "sola scriptura" (Scripture alone) is unheard of in the Orthodox tradition. Scripture is the primary basis of authority in the faith, but it must be interpreted with the help of the Holy Spirit and the wisdom of the church through the ages as collected in many of its writings. This material includes stories of martyrs, letters, sermons, and other writings from the early church, things with which most Protestant Christians are not even familiar. These writings begin in AD 96 with the First Letter of Clement and stretch for hundreds of years. This material contains the thoughts of Christians as they reflected on the faith, trying to understand what it means and how one lives it.

One story in these writings is about an early Christian named Polycarp, who is represented with icons in many Orthodox churches. He was bishop of the city of Smyrna and a leading spokesman for Christianity, and he became one of the great saints of the church. Polycarp was eighty-six years old when the persecutions by the Romans began. Christians, accused of being atheists for their refusal to worship the Roman gods, were rounded up and put to death as many of the townsfolk cheered. Polycarp was among those arrested, but no one wanted to kill him. He and the others were given the opportunity to repent of their Christianity; a simple vow to the emperor would spare them. Polycarp refused, ending a bold exchange with a proconsul by defiantly declaring, "Bring forth the fire."

The authorities lit the fire, which did not consume Polycarp at first. When it finally did, onlookers smelled the sweet scent of a sacrificial offering to God rather than the acrid stench of burning flesh. Finally, because Polycarp refused to die in those flames and was still alive and praying, the authorities drove a dagger into his heart, then burned his body.

Now, when Orthodox Christians read such stories, which are unfamiliar to us as Protestant Christians, they say, "How could you ignore these? These are stories of the witness of the saints who have gone before us!" Orthodox Christians do not literally worship icons of such saints, but they do venerate them and look to them for inspiration in standing firm as they meet their own challenges. They say, "When I am tempted to fall away from the faith, I might pray to the saint, 'Help me to have your resoluteness in claiming Christ as my Savior. Let me be a bold witness for the faith.' " You can imagine how inspirational such figures and writings could be for our Orthodox friends.

Seeing the "Real World": Liturgy, Sacred Architecture, Icons, and Prayer

There are many areas in which we would agree with the Orthodox, and a few areas where we might place a different emphasis or even disagree. For me, the most-compelling dimension of Orthodox faith and practice is the emphasis on what is ultimately real. I have had people say to me at times, "Well, this is the church; but in the real world...." The Orthodox remind us that our daily lives (our jobs, our schooling, our relationships) are not the real world. The real world is heaven, God's eternal kingdom; and real life is found in participating in that divine kingdom now, here on earth. We will spend only a small amount of time here on this earth; we are, in the words of Scripture, just pilgrims and aliens here. There is a heavenly realm that we cannot generally see. It is invisible, but it is all around us; and if we really knew and understood this, if we participated in this realm, our lives would be radically different.

How would you live differently if you knew absolutely that God was constantly by your side? How would you look at retirement, illness, pain, sorrow, and tragedy if you had actually seen heaven and knew it was more real than anything you see on this earth? How would you react to temptation if you knew that Jesus watched over you; that this life was only temporary; that the saints stood around you, cheering you on? When you are sick, or discouraged, or feeling alone, how should your faith sustain you?

Orthodoxy challenges us to live with this certainty, and much of Orthodox worship is designed to help the worshiper "see" divine reality. An Orthodox church is a building whose very purpose is to transport the worshiper to the heavenly realm. The dome we often see on the top of an Orthodox church is aimed at giving the worshiper a sense of being encompassed or embraced within that realm. The ceiling itself represents the heavens. Often a mosaic or fresco of Jesus graces the dome or ceiling, looking down on the congregation, a visible reminder that Jesus is constantly looking down on us. In this way the dome is portraying what is real.

The front of the sacred space (what we would call the chancel, what they would call the "sanctuary") is separated from the nave, where the congregation gathers during worship, by an icon screen or wall containing painted images of Jesus and his life, Mary, and the apostles. These images are teaching tools that were particularly important when people could not read. Believers could look over the various icons and learn the story of Jesus' life and reflect on its meaning. This icon wall served the same function as the curtain that separated the Holy of Holies from the rest of the Temple in Solomon's time. (You will remember that Solomon's Temple was meant to be an earthly picture of the very throne room of God. The Orthodox perceive of their buildings as fulfilling a similar function.) Behind the icon wall is the altar, which represents for

Orthodox Christians an earthly foreshadowing of a real place in the heavenly realm where God sits in judgment and rules the earth. On the side walls of this place of worship are more icons—this time of martyrs and saints who have died and have already entered God's eternal kingdom. These icons are not just reminders of people long dead, however. These icons are visible reminders that the saints are around the throne of God today and that they are praying for us and seeking to encourage us to continue to focus on Jesus and to run the race set before us.

Finally, the liturgy itself—what happens in worship—is meant to usher the worshipers into the heavenly realm, to remind them of who they are, Whose they are, and what is real. The liturgy is meant to replicate on earth the kind of worship that is taking place in heaven. It is filled with prayers of praise and thanksgiving shaped by the Scriptures and includes the reading of Scripture, chanting, a message, and the Eucharist. The use of incense is meant to remind worshipers of the glory of the Lord and to stand as a scented reminder of the prayers of God's people ascending to God. The bread and the wine of the Eucharist are a way of tasting and experiencing God. In this setting, in the scent of incense, in the use of lighting, in the sounds of the liturgy, and in the taste of the Eucharist, all senses are used to transport the worshiper to the heavenly realms.

"In Orthodox liturgy," says Father Sawchak, "we experience nothing less than heaven. We mystically join in with the angels, who are singing the Thrice Holy Hymn, 'Holy, Holy, Holy,' and with the saints of the church who have gone before us." The first half of the liturgy, the liturgy of the Word, includes readings from the Gospels and from the epistles of Paul. That is followed by the liturgy of the Eucharist, "part of which is remembering and being thankful for all of the things that have happened for us. We remember the cross, the tomb, the resurrection on the third day, the ascension into heaven, and the sitting at the right hand of the Father; and then we remember something that has already happened, and that is the second and glorious coming. We are experiencing something that has yet to happen in earthly terms but has been accomplished in mystical terms—is done and over with. We are able to fully participate, again, in nothing less than heaven."

This is the essence of faith: remembering what is true and real even though we cannot see it. This is part of what is meant to happen when any Christians gather for worship. That is, this is part of why we need weekly worship, because there we are reminded of who we are and of the reality of the kingdom of God so that we can go back into a world that will ultimately pass away and live as persons whose destination is God's eternal kingdom.

This is a gift the Orthodox give us. Since studying Orthodoxy, I have noticed how pedestrian some church sanctuaries in American Protestant churches are. I wonder if Protestant churches might not learn something from the Orthodox about sacred spaces and if we might not design worship spaces in such a way that when worshipers enter, they are receiving a foretaste of heaven, experiencing the sense of mystical communion with the saints, and seeing a vision of what the heavenly realm is like.

"Surrounded by So Great a Cloud of Witnesses..."

The one practice that most Protestants associate with the Orthodox is the veneration of icons. Icons, as we have noted, are painted figures depicting Jesus and his life, the Holy Family, angels, the apostles, and saints who have gone before us into heaven. We might see these icons not only in churches but also in the homes of the Orthodox.

"Very often," says Father Sawchak, "you find it said that icons are windows into heaven. We do not worship those who are pictured on the icons. We venerate them and we look to them—specifically, the saints of the church—as good examples to follow." He says that in a world where many people hang posters depicting movie stars or sports figures, it should not seem odd that people seeking real heroes might look to depictions of saints who may have given up their lives for Christ.

"We need good examples in our world to be able to follow and look up to," he says; "and all of those people that we look to in these icons were sinners, and they all had one common denominator: They lived a life of repentance and they changed, each in their own different way and each with different life circumstances."

My study of Orthodoxy led me to a book of the New Testament that seems very Orthodox and Eastern to me: the Epistle to the Hebrews. Hebrews was written to Jewish Christians who had experienced hardship and persecution for their faith. They had been Christians for some time, and the excitement and newness had begun to wear off. Some of them were becoming less regular in meeting together for worship. Others were allowing their spiritual passion to dim. Some, consequently, were beginning to lose their faith and were actually returning to the synagogue, where they would once again be accepted, where life might be easier.

The Book of Hebrews makes the case for these Jewish Christians to continue to follow Jesus, offering encouragement, a bit of chastisement, and some helpful advice on pursuing the Christian life. The author reminds his readers of the benefits of following Christ and the difference this makes in our lives here and for eternity.

The author of Hebrews also speaks of the earthly Temple in Jerusalem as a foreshadowing of the heavenly realm. In Hebrews 8:5 he notes of the priests in Jerusalem, "They offer worship in a sanctuary that is a sketch and shadow of the heavenly one." In Chapters 9 and 10 he continues to speak of the heavenly sanctuary of which the Temple in Jerusalem was only an earthly representation. Then the writer gives us one of the most-loved chapters in all of the New Testament, the great faith chapter. He says that this is what faith is: It is being sure of what we hope for and certain of what we do not see. This is how we live as Christians: We live by faith. We have a certainty regarding our hope in God. We trust God and we live by faith, not by what we see in this world.

Then the author recounts the faith of the heroes of the Bible. By faith, Abel offered God a better sacrifice. By faith, Noah built the ark, even though it had yet to rain a drop. By faith, Abraham answered the call of God to leave the comforts of his life and go to a land he had never seen before, living there like a stranger in a foreign country. Why did he do this? He did this because "he looked forward to the city that has foundations, whose architect and builder is God" (Hebrews 11:10). By faith, Sarah and Jacob and Joseph and Moses and Rahab and Gideon and Samson and all the rest lived, even facing persecution and death, because they were sure of what they hoped for and certain of what they could not see. Then the author brings things to a climax with these words in Chapter 12: "Therefore, since we are surrounded by so great a cloud of witnesses, let us lay aside every weight and the sin that clings so closely, and let us run with perseverance the race that is set before us, looking to Jesus the pioneer and perfecter of our faith" (Hebrews 12:1-2).

I love this! We are surrounded by this cloud of witnesses, these people of faith who trusted God and received their reward. They encircle us, they go before us, they cheer us on and challenge us not to give up the faith! I love the way so many Orthodox churches capture this feeling by lining the walls with icons of those who have gone before us. By meditating on them, by remembering what is real and what is lasting, by recalling the city whose architect and builder is God, we can throw off those things that hinder us and run with perseverance the race marked out for us.

Several years ago I entered a very old Orthodox chapel at a monastery in Greece. Its walls were covered with icons of those in the town who had died for their faith from the earliest days of Christianity. As powerful as this imagery was, I was struck by the idea that we as contemporary believers are called to be *living* icons, both in the church and in the world. We are called to be flesh-and-blood witnesses of the fact that this world we live in is only temporary and that there is a kingdom whose builder is God. We are called to encourage others as they seek to follow Jesus. And we are called to keep our eyes fixed on Jesus, the author and perfecter of our faith.

While I do not believe the Orthodox church is the only true and faithful expression of Christianity, I do believe it is one authentic expression of the Christian faith. I thank God for the richness of that faith and for all that we can learn from our Orthodox brothers and sisters.

1. Adapted from The Nicene Creed, in *The United Methodist Hymnal* (Copyright © 1989 by The United Methodist Publishing House); 880.

2. See the section on "Christ" and on "The Nature of Man" in Father Azkoul's essay, "What Are the Differences Between Orthodoxy and Roman Catholicism?" at www.ocf.org/OrthodoxPage/reading/ortho_cath.html

3. See the section on "The Development of Doctrine" at www.ocf.org/OrthodoxPage/reading/ortho_cath.html

CHAPTER 2

CATHOLICISM: SACRAMENT AND MASS

O come, let us worship and bow down,
let us kneel before the LORD, our Maker!
For he is our God,
and we are the people of his pasture,
and the sheep of his hand.
(Psalm 95:6-7)

Jesus said to them, "Very truly, I tell you, unless you eat the flesh of the Son of Man and drink his blood, you have no life in you. Those who eat my flesh and drink my blood have eternal life, and I will raise them up on the last day; for my flesh is true food and my blood is true drink. Those who eat my flesh and drink my blood abide in me, and I in them.
(John 6:53-56)

A Brief History of Catholic Christianity

Catholics make up the largest group of Christians in the world—over one billion people, as many as all Protestants and Orthodox Christians combined. In the United States, Protestants outnumber Catholics two to one; but Catholics are still twenty-three percent of the population, four times more than the next-largest denomination.

In the first century of Christianity, of course, there were no denominations as we now know them. The major division in the church was between Jewish Christians and Gentile Christians. There were no Catholics as we think of them today, no Orthodox, and no Protestants. There were only followers of the Way, as they were called, believers in Jesus Christ. Over time, as the church developed, the word *catholic*, which means "universal," was used to describe the church. It was not the name of a denomination.

When it came to early church history, all roads led to Rome. By the end of the first century, Rome was the center of the church. Peter and Paul were both put to death there. Rome was the power center of the empire and likely had the largest number of Christians of any city in the empire by the beginning of the second century. Over time, Latin came to be the dominant language of the western half of the Roman Empire; and although the New Testament was written in Greek, Latin soon came to be the language of the Western church as well.

Because of all those factors, the bishop of Rome came to be regarded as the most influential of the bishops. This is similar to the way that pastors of large and influential churches among, say, Southern Baptists tend to be highly regarded by others even though these pastors have no technical authority over other churches. In the same way, the bishop of Rome came to have influence over other churches. It was not until the end of the fourth century that the bishop of Rome came to be known as "pope," a term that simply meant "father." More telling was the fact that the bishop of Rome called the other bishops "sons." Not all of them appreciated this, but by the early fifth century the authority of the pope was generally accepted among the Western churches and grudgingly accepted by most in the Eastern churches.

Despite growing differences and tensions, the churches of the western and eastern halves of the empire remained united in their affirmation of the central tenets of the Christian faith, tenets about which these two branches of Christendom, with one key difference, still agree (See Chapter One.). The Nicene Creed of 325/381, the Apostles' Creed, and several other creeds of the early church are considered the essence of the Catholic; Orthodox; and, for that matter, Protestant faiths.

Eventually, though, these churches did split. The split became official in 1054 when the Orthodox and Catholic churches anathematized each other, and the Christian church was no longer officially united.

We have seen how Orthodox Christians see church history:

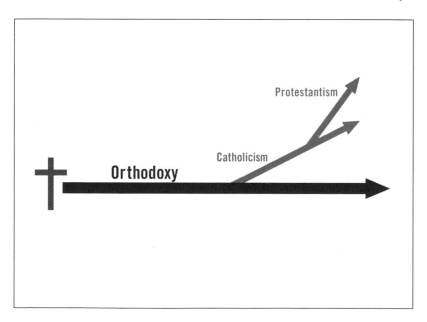

The Orthodox believe that they are the true church of the apostles and that Catholics have broken away from the faith. Catholics, of course, believe that the Roman Catholic Church is the true church of the apostles and that the Orthodox and Protestants have broken off, as illustrated here:

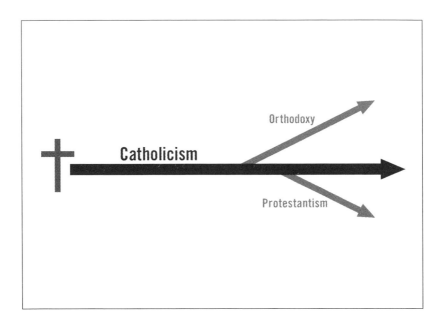

As Protestants, we agree with the essentials of the faith as articulated by our Catholic friends. Both the Nicene Creed and the Apostles' Creed are a part of our worship tradition. The differences between Catholics and Protestants arise from the traditions of the church and the doctrines that spring from them. Protestants look to the Scriptures as the primary source of faith and practice and require that any doctrine or required practice of the faith be closely related to the text of Scripture. Catholics also look to the Bible as the source of faith and practice, but they hold that the Holy Spirit did not cease to guide the church into truth with the death of the apostles. Like the Orthodox, Catholics believe that the Holy Spirit continued to reveal truth and doctrine through the bishops, theologians, and councils of the church as they reflected on the Scriptures. Hence, there are some practices and doctrines dear to Catholics that are difficult for Protestants to see plainly in the Scriptures. Catholics argue that the seeds of these doctrines are in the Scriptures, although the more obscure these "seeds," the less likely Protestants are to accept them.

"The doctrine in the church found in Holy Scripture and Apostolic Tradition," according to Dr. Claude Sasso, vice-chancellor of the diocese of Kansas City and Saint Joseph and a respected Catholic educator, "what we call the 'deposit of faith,' is something that is given by Christ and guaranteed by the Holy Spirit. Christ said in his prayer and in his discussion with the apostles that all truth would be brought to mind by the Holy Spirit." Jesus' guarantee of the Holy Spirit meant that this "deposit of faith" was passed along orally before being written into the New Testament, whose canon, Dr. Sasso reminds us, was not even finally defined until the Council of Rome in 382. As with other practices and doctrines, it was the bishops of the church, led by the Spirit, who determined which books would be included in the New Testament. Catholics note that the idea that the Bible, apart from the tradition of the church (the pronouncements of councils and bishops and theologians), should be the only source of the doctrines of the faith ignores the promise of Jesus that the Holy Spirit would guide the church. And it ignores the fact that there would be no New Testament as we have it were it not for the work of the bishops and councils!

One example of the different ways Protestants and Catholics look at sources for faith and practice is the Roman Catholic Church's teaching about Mary. Protestants affirm all that is found in the New Testament regarding Mary and honor her as the mother of our Lord. Catholics start with the Scriptures, but they also look to the traditions and theological arguments that developed around Mary through the centuries to affirm doctrines that Protestants do not accept; namely, that she was immaculately conceived, was perpetually a virgin, and was assumed into heaven at her death (her body not being subject to decay). The difference here is that Protestants do not find sufficient support in Scripture for these doctrines, while Catholics find seeds of the doctrines in the New Testament and cite what they believe to be Holy Spirit-led traditions and teachings of the church through the centuries as pointing toward the truth of these doctrines.

Several years ago I had the opportunity to read the *Roman Catholic Catechism,* the official teachings of the Roman Catholic Church. I was surprised by how much Roman Catholics and Protestants agree on. We agree on the tenets of the faith as expressed in the Nicene and Apostles' creeds. We agree that the Bible is our primary guide to faith and practice. We agree that Jesus Christ is the Savior of the world. Catholics who take seriously the teachings of their church will find themselves pursuing a rich spiritual life in which Jesus Christ is Lord.

Catholicism has changed over the centuries. It is not uncommon today to find adult Bible studies, vacation Bible school for children, and even Protestant hymns used in Catholic churches. And, to the surprise of some Catholics, increasingly there is an appreciation within Protestant churches for some historic Catholic practices. In this chapter, rather than focus on the issues that divide Catholics and Protestants, we will look at three areas of Catholic practice that Protestants would do well to learn from: ritual, reverence, and the Eucharist.

Roman Catholic Beliefs and Practices

The Power of Ritual

Protestants, since the time of the Reformation, have had a tendency to throw out ritual as something dead and devoid of meaning. Reacting to what was perceived as a gospel nearly obscured by empty ritualism, Protestants jettisoned nearly all ritual. Over time we have come to understand what a bad decision that was. Ritual does not have to be dead and empty; it can be powerful and life giving. It can shape our lives, provide discipline, and help us integrate our faith into our daily routines. Here Catholics have much to teach us. They have, for instance, helped Protestants understand the power of observing the various seasons of the Christian year. I have come to appreciate the importance of Advent (the four weeks leading up to Christmas) as a season of preparation and spiritual focus in the midst of rampant commercialism. I have come to love Ash Wednesday services as we repent of our sins and enter the forty days of Lent, a time of fasting and intensified spiritual focus in our walk with Jesus toward his cross and resurrection.

Catholic devotional practices such as praying the Stations of the Cross (a way of recalling the story of the passion and death of Jesus) are becoming increasingly valued in Protestant churches. Some Protestants have begun developing their own versions of the Stations of the Cross taken directly from Scripture.

The rosary is another element of Roman Catholic ritual from which Protestants might learn. It is a tool used to recount the stories of Mary and Jesus while offering scriptural words of affirmation and prayer. The rosary includes the "Hail Mary" taken from Luke's Gospel; the Lord's Prayer; the Apostles' Creed; and the recounting of the story of Jesus' life, death, and resurrection. While Protestants might reject those few portions of the rosary devoted to extra-biblical stories and the repeating of words of affirmation to Mary, the idea of daily making use of this tool to pray, worship, and recount the Gospel stories would not be inconsistent with Protestant devotional practice.

A couple of years ago, I spent three days in a Benedictine monastery, in complete silence except when I joined the monks in the chapel for worship, which involved praying the psalms, or for a meal and discussion following the service. The rest of the time was spent in silence, reading, praying, or working. The rhythm of these rituals began to shape my soul in very positive ways. Many Protestants have been welcomed and have discovered profound spiritual experiences in Roman Catholic monasteries.

Reverence for the Sacred

A second lesson Protestants can learn from Catholics is the importance of reverence for sacred things. Many of us as Protestants have lost our sense of the sacred. We often fail to demonstrate appropriate respect for God. We treat holy things as though they were profane. There are Protestants who, when finished with Holy Communion, pour the remaining wine or juice down the drain in the kitchen sink. Catholics would find this unthinkable; this wine has been consecrated. It is holy; it is Christ's blood. If the wine is not completely consumed by the congregation and priests, it is to be poured into the ground, just as Christ's blood fell to the ground. The consecrated bread is saved in the tabernacle or fed to the birds; it is never thrown away.

In their worship Catholics express reverence with their entire bodies. I find powerful the idea of bowing the knee when facing the place where the body of Christ is kept. I love the way, when the Gospel is read, Catholics make the sign of the cross on their forehead, lips, and heart, saying, "The Gospel be on my mind, and on my lips, and in my heart." Likewise, I appreciate the idea of crossing oneself when the name of the Trinity is pronounced, as a way of saying, "Father, Son, and Holy Spirit, I am yours. Cover me, fill me, have me." Standing, kneeling, and crossing are opportunities to demonstrate respect and an appropriate sense of reverence and awe. These actions are, to Catholics, what the raising of hands in worship is to Pentecostals.

The passage from the Book of Psalms at the beginning of this chapter is one of many that call God's people to humble themselves before God, to bow or kneel or tremble before the Lord. We recall from the Hebrew Bible that the glory and holiness of God were such that any Israelite who even touched the ark of the covenant died. Anyone who entered the Temple when the glory of the Lord had filled that place would die. God is holy and is to be revered. We Protestants often see Jesus as our friend, which is true; but Catholics help us remember that God is also holy and to be respected and that our divine friend is also the King of kings and Lord of lords and thus worthy of our reverence.

The Power of the Eucharist

We come now to what is perhaps the single most-important spiritual practice of Catholic Christians, one in which we see both ritual and reverence: the Eucharist.

At his last Passover supper with his disciples, Jesus broke the bread; gave thanks for it; and gave new meaning to the Passover meal, saying that the bread and wine were his body and blood, given to initiate a new covenant with God, offering forgiveness and salvation. He commanded his disciples, as often as they did this, to remember him. It seems likely to me that in the early church, at least every week, Christians remembered with a meal of bread and wine the Lord's death and his presence with them.

Some Christians believe that, just as the Passover was held once a year to commemorate God's salvation of the Jews, so the Lord's Supper should be held annually, at the time of Jesus' death, to commemorate his saving work for us. Others believe that Jesus was teaching, at the Last Supper, that whenever the disciples ate a meal together, they were to remember him. Some believe this meal should be shared from time to time as a way of recalling Jesus' death. Others believe the Lord's Supper is more than a memorial of his death; it is also a way in which Christians receive his grace and therefore should be celebrated monthly or weekly.

For Catholics, the Eucharist is the point of the entire service of worship. It is the climactic conclusion and the most-important part of what happens when they gather for worship.

In the Roman Catholic tradition, according to Dr. Sasso, "the Eucharist is God's presence. At a Holy Mass, when the priest says the words of Christ and gives an invocation, or prayer, to the Holy Spirit to change the substance of the bread and wine, we believe that although these elements do not change in their appearance, or their 'accidents,' their actual substances will change, so that what we receive is really Christ's presence. It is his sacrifice and his blood from which all grace flows, and that is why we say the Eucharist is the source and summit of the Catholic faith: because it is Christ himself—body, blood, soul, and divinity—that we receive. I want to offer him my life. I want to surrender it to him; and if I do that, I feel that my communion is much more blessed. In the sacrifice of the Mass, it is Christ's sacrifice which is re-presented; the sacrifice Christ offered once for all on the cross remains ever present."

Catholics believe that in the midst of the prayer offered by the priest, the bread and wine actually become the body and blood of Christ. This is a doctrine called "transubstantiation." Generally, Protestants have rejected this idea. Yet here the Catholics, rather than the Protestants, are taking the Bible literally; for this is a very literal reading of what Jesus said in John 6 when he spoke of eating his flesh and drinking his blood. It is also a literal reading of what Paul says in 1 Corinthians 11:29: "For all who eat and drink without discerning the body, eat and drink judgment against themselves." Did Jesus and Paul have in mind the doctrine of transubstantiation? Protestants do not think so, and they interpret these words to mean receiving the symbols of bread and wine as representing the body and blood of Christ. Catholics believe Jesus and Paul did intend to teach transubstantiation and that these passages are to be taken literally; and it is true that very early in the history of the church, Christians embraced this idea.

While most Protestants do not believe the bread and wine are actually changed into the body and blood of Christ, most do believe that Christ is truly present in the bread and the wine and that by receiving them we are, spiritually, receiving Christ himself. This meal is a tangible expression of his presence. In this meal we have an opportunity, in a physical way, to express our acceptance of Christ's gift of salvation. We communicate our need for his mercy, we physically receive him, and we experience God's grace in the eating of this meal.

When I receive the Eucharist, I kneel before the Lord and humbly confess that I need the salvation he offers. I acknowledge that he was crucified for my sins. Like Dr. Sasso, when I come to the Lord's Table, I am surrendering my life to Christ; and this is what I hope you experience and intend when you receive this meal.

This meal binds us together as Christians; it celebrates and commemorates the suffering, death, and resurrection of Christ; it is a tangible way to humble ourselves before God and to accept once again his saving work; and it feeds our souls. Ignatius of Antioch, writing in AD 107 on his way to martyrdom, described the Eucharist as "the medicine of immortality, the antidote against death," not the mindless eating of a wafer and drinking of wine, but the receiving of the life of Christ.

There are points on which Protestants and Catholics will always disagree (We will consider some of these points in the next chapter as we look at Lutheranism.). However, there are far more points of faith and practice about which we agree. I believe Catholics have much to gain from a greater openness to Protestants, but I also believe that Protestants have much to gain from a greater openness to Catholics. Protestants have taught and continue to teach our Catholic friends about the power of preaching and the importance of Bible study, as well as about the joy of building community through small groups, the power of hymns and songs of praise, the role of the laity in ministry, and an openness to women in the pastorate—the Catholic Church since Vatican II in particular has drawn upon these traditions of Protestantism. But Protestants also have much to learn from our Catholic friends about the importance of ritual, the role of reverence, the power of the Eucharist, and a great deal more.

I do not believe that Protestants and Catholics will ever unite under the leadership of Rome, nor do I believe that Orthodox Christians will agree to this. But I do believe we might all look at one another as authentic followers of Jesus Christ—as different as the various disciples but all with a heart to serve the Lord; all a part of the one holy, catholic, and apostolic church.

CHAPTER 3

LUTHERANISM: WORD AND FAITH

But now, apart from law, the righteousness of God has been disclosed, and is attested by the law and the prophets, the righteousness of God through faith in Jesus Christ for all who believe. For there is no distinction, since all have sinned and fall short of the glory of God; they are now justified by his grace as a gift, through the redemption that is in Christ Jesus.

(Romans 3:21-24)

Come to him, a living stone, though rejected by mortals yet chosen and precious in God's sight, and like living stones, let yourselves be built into a spiritual house, to be a holy priesthood, to offer spiritual sacrifices acceptable to God through Jesus Christ.

(1 Peter 2:4-5)

A Brief History of Lutheranism

A Church in Need of Reform

To understand and appreciate Martin Luther and the Protestant Reformation, we must first understand the state of Christianity in Luther's time. A word picture might be helpful:

Imagine yourself walking from Kansas City toward Denver without a compass or roads to follow. You may know that Denver is virtually due west of Kansas City, so all you have to do is keep going straight. But what would happen if you got off track, ever so slightly—let's say by just a few degrees—and you never figured out what you had done? It would hardly be noticeable at first. But the farther you traveled, the greater the difference would become and the farther off course you would be. Finally, rather than arriving in Denver, you might find yourself in Cheyenne, Wyoming.

In the view of Luther, the same was true of the church. Changes that might have seemed minor at first had taken the church farther and farther off track as the years went on, until finally the differences became significant. In the years leading up to Luther's protest, the church experienced perhaps her darkest period ever. That darkness was not the result of persecutions or threats but rather of the church losing her way. She had gotten off course.

You might think this is simply a Protestant view, but here is an excerpt from the *Catholic Encyclopedia* (a comprehensive guide for Catholics who wish to learn more about the faith) dealing with the church in the century leading up to the birth of Martin Luther:

> Gradually a regrettable worldliness manifested itself in many high ecclesiastics. Their chief object—to guide man to his eternal goal—claimed too seldom their attention.... Many bishops and abbots (especially in countries where they were also territorial princes) bore themselves as secular rulers rather than as servants of the Church. Many members of cathedral chapters and other...ecclesiastics were chiefly concerned with their income and how to increase

it.... Luxury prevailed widely among the higher clergy.... The scientific and ascetic training of the clergy left much to be desired, the moral standard of many being very low, and the practice of celibacy not everywhere observed.... As to the Christian people itself, in numerous districts ignorance, superstition, religious indifference, and immorality were rife.... From the fourteenth century the demand for "reform of head and members"... had been voiced with ever-increasing energy by serious and discerning men.[1]

Luther's Struggle and Course of Action

This was the state of the church when Martin Luther was ordained a priest in 1507. But it was his personal, spiritual, and emotional struggle, what he called *anfechtungen*, that moved him to desperation in his search for a God of mercy. Luther had been reared with the fear of God. Jesus was a judge from whom he felt nothing but condemnation. This, coupled with what some believe was a persistent struggle with depression, led Luther to occasional bouts of despair. He was overwhelmed with guilt and felt alienated from a God he could not please. His despair was at times nearly overwhelming, and this struggle led Luther to search for grace.

It would take several decades for Luther finally to formulate what became the hallmark idea of the reformation he would lead: Human beings are justified or made right with God not by our works, but by God's work in Jesus Christ. Luther found this message in the gospel as the apostle Paul described it, particularly in Romans, where Paul wrote, "But now, apart from law, the righteousness of God has been disclosed, and is attested by the law and the prophets, the righteousness of God through faith in Jesus Christ for all who believe. For there is no distinction, since all have sinned and fall short of the glory of God; they are now justified by his grace as a gift, through the redemption that is in Christ Jesus" (Romans 3:21-24).

As Luther began to find peace and joy in the gospel of grace, he also came to be increasingly troubled by what he observed in the Roman Catholic Church into which he was ordained. The abuse that ultimately served as the trigger for his protest against the Catholicism of his day was the selling of indulgences. The pope was raising funds to erect Saint Peter's Cathedral in Rome. To do so, a number of preachers were commissioned to conduct what in essence was a capital funds campaign. Most of the people they petitioned would never see the cathedral in Rome, but a powerful spiritual and theological incentive was offered as a way of coaxing them to give. The preachers told people that contributing to this effort would result in prayers offered on behalf of a loved one, in which the church would petition God to accept these acts of devotion (the giving of monetary gifts toward the construction of Saint Peter's and the prayers for the departed loved one) as a way of ensuring that the loved one would spend less time in Purgatory. One of these preachers, a man named Tetzel, came and spoke in Luther's town.

Tetzel, in a sermon encouraging his listeners to place money in the coffer, was quoted as saying, "Don't you hear the voices of your wailing dead parents and others who say, 'Have mercy upon me, have mercy upon me, because we are in severe punishment and pain. From this you could redeem us with a small alms and yet you do not want to do so.' "[2]

This kind of preaching infuriated Luther and led him to compose a list of ninety-five statements questioning the practice of indulgences and the state of the church in his day. He posted these statements, or "theses," on the doors of the Castle Church in Wittenberg, Germany. The date was October 31,

1517, what many call Halloween but what Lutherans call Reformation Day. Luther's Ninety-five Theses were reproduced on a relatively new invention, the printing press; and soon his challenge to the church and its practices was spread across the land.

Luther expressed in his writings the frustration that many people, especially among the middle and upper classes, were feeling with regard to the state of the church and its abuses. In particular, he felt that, while the clergy will always play an important role in the church, all men and women can come directly to God through Christ without the intervention of a priest. As Luther expressed it, "We have no priest save Christ himself."

When the church refused to acknowledge its abuses, and instead sought to silence Luther, there was a break from the Roman Catholic Church, which Luther deemed apostate; and the Protestant branch of Christianity was born, beginning a movement that came to be called the Protestant Reformation.

Within a relatively short period of time, Lutheranism came to be the church of large portions of Germany, Denmark, Sweden, and Norway.

We should note here that both Luther and John Calvin, about whom we will read in the next chapter, were magisterial reformers—that is, their reforms were supported by magistrates, or ruling authorities. With all the reforms they brought about, neither Luther nor Calvin changed his views on church and state; to be a citizen of the state was to be baptized into the Christian church. Church and state continued to be linked.

We have seen how various churches envision the history of Christianity, with Orthodox Christians taking this view:

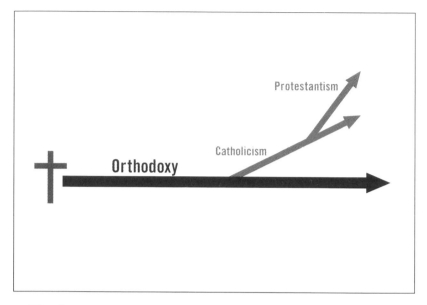

The Orthodox believe that they are the true preservers of the faith and that Catholics and Protestants have deviated from the truth.

Catholics see church history like this:

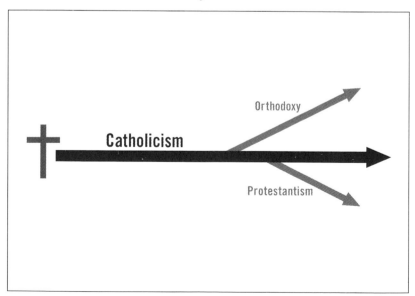

In this view Catholics have maintained the true faith, and Orthodox and Protestant believers have deviated from the path. But this is how Lutherans see the course of church history:

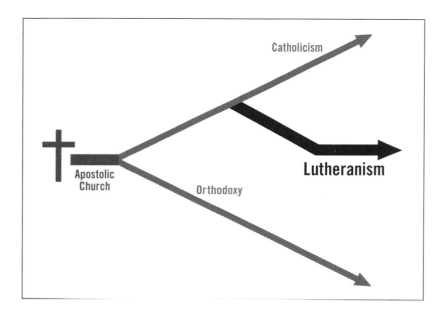

Lutherans believe that both Catholic and Orthodox Christians had gotten off course, ever so slightly, perhaps beginning not long after Christianity became the official religion of the Roman Empire. Over the next thousand years, these small deviations from the faith of the apostles resulted in a church that was lost. Luther saw himself seeking to move the Roman Catholic Church back to the path of the apostles in what amounted to a mid-course correction.

Today there are 82.6 million Lutherans around the world, including 13.6 million members of several different Lutheran denominations in America[3]; and they continue to preach and teach the gospel in much the same way that Luther did nearly five hundred years ago. I would like to lift up three of the most-important beliefs put forth by Luther in the Reformation and held by Lutheran Christians. You will notice that these ideas are also central emphases in many other Protestant churches.

Lutheran Beliefs and Practices

The Priesthood of All Believers

When Luther spoke of the priesthood of all believers, "he was really talking about the vocation to which each and every Christian is called," says Bishop Gerald Mansholt, Bishop of the Central States Synod of the Evangelical Lutheran Church of America. "It meant that everyone who follows Jesus is called to use the gifts that God has given in our life's ministry in the world. To be a Christian, one does not need to go and live in a monastery or be ordained to serve as a pastor or bishop in a church.

"Luther also understood that worship was meant for the whole people of God. In Luther's day, much of worship was centered on what the priest did at the front of the church in the liturgy. Luther translated hymns and the Scriptures into the language of the people and wrote hymns so that people might sing their praises to God. He tried to lift up the whole people of God and to help them to live out their lives in their faith and in their calling."

Luther maintained that all believers were ordained, in their baptism, to serve God and to do God's work. This is where joy is found: in responding to God's call. Luther believed that every day, in everything we do, we can respond to God's call on our life. Certainly this includes ministry in the church. But this also includes our daily life. What happens when we come to see our workplace as a mission field and the people there as being in need of Christ's love? What happens when we begin to look at our neighbors and ask, "How can I be in ministry with them and share the love of Christ in tangible ways?"

One young man I knew took this calling seriously. He had a neighbor who was a bit obnoxious. She had complained about him and his children to others. She even called the city codes department to report him for not having an extension on one of the downspouts of his house. But when this woman's husband died, the young man went to the funeral. He prayed daily for her. He began mowing her lawn. He reported that mowing the woman's lawn became a source of blessing to him and a way of serving not just the woman, but God. In the process the young man's ministry to his neighbor changed her heart, and she could not look at him the same way again.

I think similarly about the people in my congregation who have taken ministry seriously. A small group in the church has been working with an inner-city ministry, providing hope to people in need. One of our senior adults delivers fifteen coffee mugs a week to first-time visitors to our church in order to welcome them to our congregation. Another member is at the church every week welcoming people, serving wherever there is a need. Still another, a man in his forties with small children at home, helps organize our food drives and grocery rebate program, which distribute tons of food to low-income people in Kansas City. Recently I walked into our church's foyer to see two hundred of our members at a music ministries retreat. God has given them the gift of music, and they are seeking to honor him and minister to others.

God intends that we understand ourselves to be in ministry. This is what we read in 1 Peter 2:4-5: "Come to him, a living stone, though rejected by mortals yet chosen and precious in God's sight, and like living stones, let yourselves be built into a spiritual house, to be a holy priesthood, to offer spiritual sacrifices acceptable to God through Jesus Christ." It is what Paul tells us in Ephesians 4:11-12 when he says that pastors are to prepare *God's people* for the work of ministry. It is what Jesus had in mind when he told us that we are to live as salt and light in the world (Matthew 5:13-16). And there is a tremendous joy in this kind of service!

Where are you serving? Look around in your own church. Ask and you will see opportunities and needs that exist right now. Among the legacies of Luther's Reformation is the understanding that you have been ordained as a minister for God.

Sola Scriptura

Luther's second central affirmation is what is known as "sola scriptura," Scripture alone. Luther came to believe that the Bible was the primary authority in defining the faith and practice of Christians, not the pope or the councils or the church. He believed that Christians were to read the Bible and interpret it with the help of the Holy Spirit. This stood in stark contrast to the church of his day, which taught that giving the Bible to the laity was dangerous and therefore the Bible was to be read and interpreted only by the pope and clergy.

Furthermore, Luther said that if a doctrine could not be demonstrated from the Scriptures, it could not be made binding on the church. This was a radical rejection of the role of the church in shaping doctrine, and it led to a rejection of many of the practices of the Roman Catholic Church. Luther saw the New Testament as defining what Christ and the apostles felt the faith was supposed to look like. He could not find in the New Testament the doctrine that priests and pastors could not marry. In fact, he saw that Peter, the great apostle of the church, was married; and so he determined that forbidding clergy to marry was a nonbiblical doctrine. At the age of forty-one, Luther married a former nun who also had come to believe that marriage was not against God's will for clergy.

A sacrament was defined in Luther's day as an act specifically commanded by Christ that communicated the grace of God. When Luther read the New Testament, he found not seven sacraments, but two that were commanded by the Lord: baptism and the Eucharist. Luther considered other practices as potentially helpful but refused to consider them sacraments. In the same way, he began to measure all church doctrine and practice against what the New Testament clearly taught; and that which was not drawn from the New Testament was deemed nonbinding on the believer.

The most-important thing Luther did in this regard was to teach and encourage others to read and study the Bible and to preach the Word, which offered life. This was the second great legacy of the Reformation: placing the Bible in the hands of the laity and encouraging them to read it and live by it.

All this leads me to ask, Are you studying the Scriptures? Do you know your Bible? Luther was stunned to find the number of Christians in his day who did not know the Lord's Prayer, the Ten Commandments, or the Apostles' Creed. He devised what is known as the *Smaller Catechism* as a tool to help believers begin to know the basics of the faith.

Justification by Faith

Luther grew up with a conception of salvation that left him afraid and without peace. He was taught that human beings are sinners and that our salvation hinges on our doing enough good works to overshadow our sins. Afraid of God, Luther continually tried to please him but never felt assurance. Then, as Luther studied Paul's letters to the Romans and Galatians, he happened on an insight that would utterly transform his relationship with God.

"In the midst of Luther's own struggles," says Bishop Mansholt, "he came to the insight that we are made right with God not on the basis of what we do or what we bring. It is not that we somehow merit salvation, but that salvation is the working of God and God's gift to us in Jesus Christ."

To Luther this insight was so plain in the Scriptures, yet it was utterly alien to the time in which he lived. In the end it became a central tenet of Luther's faith and the entire Protestant Reformation. We know it as the doctrine of "justification by faith."

Luther described this kind of faith in his preface to the Book of Romans:

> Faith is God's work in us, that changes us and gives new birth from God. (John 1:13). It kills the Old Adam and makes us completely different people. It changes our hearts, our spirits, our thoughts and all our powers. It brings the Holy Spirit with it. Yes, it is a living, creative, active and powerful thing, this faith.... Faith is a living, bold trust in God's grace, so certain of God's favor that it would risk death a thousand times trusting in it. Such confidence and knowledge of God's grace makes you happy, joyful and bold in your relationship to God and all creatures. The Holy Spirit makes this happen through faith.[4]

This idea, that we are justified by God's grace through our faith and not by our works, was liberating not only for Luther but also for countless millions. Some two hundred years after Luther penned the above words, John Wesley described the effect they had on him:

In the evening I went very unwillingly to a society in Aldersgate Street, where one was reading Luther's preface to the Epistle to the Romans. About a quarter before nine, while he was describing the change which God works in the heart through faith in Christ, I felt my heart strangely warmed. I felt I did trust in Christ, Christ alone, for salvation; and an assurance was given me that He had taken away my sins, even mine, and saved me from the law of sin and death.[5]

Luther had grown up feeling that he must please God by his works and that God was a righteous and angry judge. He came to see that God is a God of love and mercy and that the response required from us as Christians is simply to trust in this love. There is a tremendous difference between these two kinds of faith.

Allow me to illustrate: Perhaps you or someone you know was reared in a home where one or both parents never seemed to express love or affirmation, or did so only conditionally (for example, if you performed well enough in school or athletics). You can imagine that people reared in such a way would devote a lot of time and energy to trying to please their parents—even as adults—longing to win the parents' affirmation, which seldom comes. Contrast such parents with those who love their children unconditionally, parents whose love and affirmation are readily given to their children so that the children never wonder if their parents love them.

Similarly, in the Catholicism of Luther's day, God's love was, at least for some, conditional. As a result, Luther and many others were left feeling that they could never quite measure up to or win God's love or affirmation. But what Luther came to see was that God, in Jesus Christ, had already expressed his love and mercy towards us: He had saved us and demonstrated his love for us. Our only task is to accept this love, by faith; to trust in it and live in grateful response to this mercy.

Which leads me to one last story. Several years ago, my wife and I finally took our daughter Danielle to college. It was a day we had been dreading since her first day of kindergarten. For me, it turned out that the actual day was not nearly as bad as her last night at home. That evening I had told Danielle to call me when she was ready for bed so I could come and tell her good night one last time before she moved away from home. It was just before midnight, and I sat down on the floor in her bedroom. I said, "There are just a few last things I want to say to you before you move away." I started to tell her how deeply her mother and I love her; and with that, sitting on her floor, I started sobbing. We spoke for thirty minutes or so; and then I knelt next to her bed and prayed for her future and for God's protection and blessings for her, crying all the way through the prayer.

When I hear Jesus saying that God is like our Father, I think of the unconditional love I felt that night and try to imagine how much greater God's love for us must be. God's love is not predicated on whether we are "good enough." Instead, we are meant to live as those who know we are loved. We rest in that love. We find joy in that love. I think this is what Luther was experiencing and trying to convey when he came to understand that we are justified by faith.

Ministry is not just the domain of the clergy; it is what each of us is called to do. Joy, meaning, and fulfillment come in pursuing God's calling on our lives. The Bible offers us the compass by which we live. Through it, God speaks to all of us; and our Christian life will be incomplete apart from studying and listening to his Word. We are saved by God's grace, not by our works; and we are called simply to accept and trust in

God's gift of love and life. These are some of the legacies of Luther's ministry, and they are still championed by our Lutheran friends. Luther's ideas would be picked up by others who would press them further, including a reformer named John Calvin. It is to his work and that of his spiritual descendants that we now turn.

1. From www.newadvent.org/cathen/12700b.htm—the Catholic Encyclopedia online—in its article "The Reformation."

2. From *Dokumente zum Ablassstreit,* by W. Köhler; pages 125-26.

3. From Wikipedia at www.en.wikipedia.org/wiki/Lutheran.

4. From "An Introduction to St. Paul's Letter to the Romans," in Luther's German Bible of 1522 by Martin Luther; translated by Reverend Robert E. Smith.

5. From *The Works of John Wesley,* edited by Albert C. Outler (Abingdon Press, 1988); Vol. 18; entry for May 24, 1738.

CHAPTER 4

PRESBYTERIANISM: THE SOVEREIGNTY OF GOD

For I know that my Redeemer lives,
*   and that at the last he will stand upon the earth;*
and after my skin has been thus destroyed,
*   then in my flesh I shall see God,*
whom I shall see on my side,
*   and my eyes shall behold, and not another.*
                                        (Job 19:25-27a)

In your book were written
*   all the days that were formed for me,*
*   when none of them as yet existed.*
How weighty to me are your thoughts, O God!
*   How vast is the sum of them!*
I try to count them—they are more than the sand;
*   I come to the end—I am still with you.*
                                        (Psalm 139:16b-18)

We know that all things work together for good for those
who love God, who are called according to his purpose.
                                        (Romans 8:28)

A Brief History of Presbyterianism

Shortly after Martin Luther led the initial revolt against the abuses of the Roman Catholic Church of his day, other reformers began making similar calls for change, in turn garnering their own followers. The proliferation of this process in centuries to come was one tragic outcome of Luther's assertion that the Bible is the primary source of faith and practice and that individual Christians can interpret it apart from the church. Christian leaders who disagreed with one another on minor points of doctrine formed their own churches or denominations. The result was a seemingly endless line of disputes and disagreements, often about small matters of theology, that led to the splintering and fracturing of the Christian church into thousands of Protestant denominations and as many as 35,000 independent nondenominational churches in the United States alone.[1]

Most early reformers agreed with Luther's essential claims, but many felt he had not gone far enough in calling for reform of or separation from Catholic practice. Disagreements arose regarding the nature of the Eucharist, or Holy Communion; the forms of worship; and how much of sixteenth-century Catholicism needed to be rejected. If you attend a Lutheran church service today, you will find that the worship is much closer to Catholicism than that of Protestant denominations from the next wave of reformers. John Calvin and his protégé John Knox were among that second wave, and their efforts resulted in the formation of the Reformed and Presbyterian churches. (Swiss, Dutch, and some German groups used the name "Reformed," while Scotch and English groups used the name "Presbyterian.") Knox played a key role in forming the Church of Scotland, which Presbyterians view as their mother church; but Calvin is seen as the theological father of both the Presbyterian and Reformed traditions. So we will focus a bit on Calvin's beliefs in this chapter.

Presbyterian—*Presbuteros*—"Elders"

First, we might note where the name "Presbyterian" comes from. We learned that "Orthodox" is a name that means "right worship" and "right doctrine." "Catholic" means universal, and with that name the Roman Catholic Church was claiming to be the one universal church. Lutherans, much to Martin Luther's chagrin, took their name from him, as followers of his reform movement. But Presbyterians draw their name from the way they are organized, adapting the Greek New Testament word for "elder": *presbuteros.* Presbyterians are those whose form of church organization does not include bishops but rather includes elders who lead each local congregation.

"We, as Presbyterians," says Doug Rumford, a pastor in the Presbyterian Church of America, "really emphasize the responsibility of the people of God. Our board is made up of teaching elders, known as pastors, and ruling elders, known simply as elders. And really, the business of the church is conducted in many ways by the ministry of the laity."

As we have seen, Lutherans believe that Catholicism and Orthodoxy strayed from the true apostolic faith, slightly at first, but with a trajectory that took them far from the path over hundreds of years. Luther sought to reform the church and restore her. We learned in the last chapter that this is how Lutherans see church history:

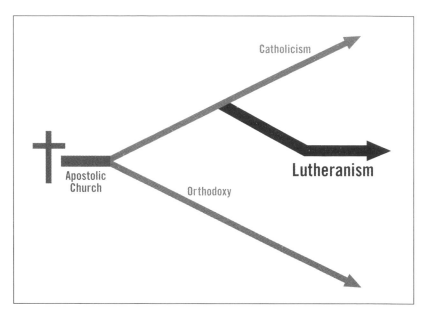

Presbyterians felt Luther had not gone quite far enough, and so their view of church history might look something like this:

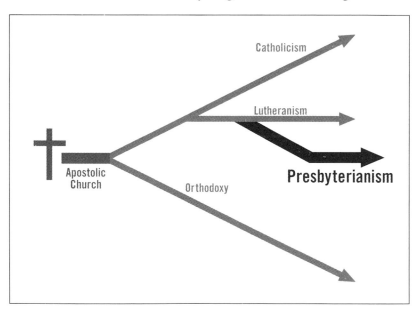

Presbyterian and Reformed churches have sought to restore the church to the path of the apostles. The leaders in the early Reformed movement, while expressing great appreciation for Luther, sought to lead the church still closer to the biblical church of the apostles.

John Calvin

John Calvin, born in 1509, was eight years old when Luther posted his Ninety-five Theses on the doors of the Castle Church at Wittenberg, signaling the beginning of the Reformation. Calvin studied law in Paris and in his early twenties had a conversion experience. At age twenty-five he left Paris for Basel, Switzerland, where he became an avowed Protestant seeking the reform of the church. A year later, he wrote the first edition of *Institutes of the Christian Religion,* perhaps the single most-important book published during the Reformation, and a book he would continue to revise for the next twenty-five years.

Among the qualities I appreciate about Presbyterians is their emphasis on both Bible study and the intellect. Dr. Rumford says Presbyterians tend to be a bit "cerebral," loving God enthusiastically with their minds.

"Presbyterians experience God first of all by that touch of grace," he says; "and many, if they don't have a moment of conversion, will have a moment of recognition, when they realize 'I really love the Lord.' Secondly, Presbyterians love God with their minds. We love the idea that 'You shall love the Lord your God with all your heart, mind, soul, and strength.' We *really* love God with our minds. And that means we love ideas and theology and meditation and reflection and the creeds of the faith, and we experience God often by encountering God through his Word."

Among the distinctive beliefs of historic Presbyterianism were five theological points known by the acronym TULIP. Although some Presbyterians today take a bit more-moderate stance on these ideas, others hold fast to them. These five points of Calvinism are as follows:

T – Total depravity, which means that we human beings are utterly sinful. Like those who are dead, we cannot resurrect or save ourselves. We are so lost and broken by original sin that we cannot even turn toward God.

U – Unconditional election is Calvin's doctrine of predestina-tion: his belief that God has chosen, from the foundation of the world, some to be saved and others to be damned. Those who are chosen for salvation were picked not on the basis of any-thing they had done, but solely on the basis of God's choice. There is nothing about us that merits this election.

L – Limited atonement teaches that Christ's death brought salvation not for all, but only for the elect: those whom God chose and predestined to receive salvation.

I – Irresistible grace says that if you are among the chosen or elect of God, you cannot refuse God's salvation; your will has nothing to do with your salvation. You will be unable to resist God's grace.

P – Perseverance of the saints means that the elect cannot lose their salvation. Once you are saved—which, if you are among the elect, will take place—you cannot slip away; you will perse-vere in your faith until the Day of Judgment. If you do slip away from God, it is likely that you were not really one of the elect.

It is this point of predestination, and several of its corollar-ies, that has been the major sticking point between Presbyterians and some other Protestant groups over the last three hundred years.

The Sovereignty of God—God's Reign

Let's turn now to one of the hallmarks of Presbyterian and Reformed theology: the sovereignty of God. It would be difficult to talk with a Presbyterian for long without this phrase coming up. The word *sovereignty*, with regard to God, is a way of saying that God is the absolute ruler, reigning over every aspect of creation; and the concept is, according to Dr. Rumford, a "primary emphasis" of Presbyterians.

"It comes out in doctrines such as election and predestination," he says; "but what it means, really, is that God's will will be done. God is God, and we are not; and even though we may not understand everything, we trust God's heart. So when my head can't grasp it, my heart maintains a tremendous trust in who God is."

Calvin, in his seminal work *Institutes of the Christian Religion,* is clear that nothing happens apart from the will of God. Even the evil that human beings do, while committed by the individual, is in some way directed as a part of God's plans. Calvin ends Book I of *Institutes* with a chapter called "The instrumentality of the wicked employed by God, while he continues free from every taint," in which Calvin writes, "That men do nothing save at the secret instigation of God, and do not discuss and deliberate on anything but what he has previously decreed with himself, and brings to pass by his secret direction, is proved by numberless clear passages of Scripture."

There is a sense in which this doctrine brings great comfort and hope to some Presbyterians and Reformed Christians and those influenced by them. It means that no matter how awful things may be, God is at work. Our lives are not subject to chance. God's purposes are being unfolded or revealed, even if we cannot see them now; for there is absolutely nothing that happens that is outside of God's will.

This doctrine raises questions for some Christians, however. In the aftermath of Hurricane Katrina, I spoke to Dr. Tom Are, Senior Pastor of Village Presbyterian Church, in Prairie Village, Kansas, asking if he believed God had decreed this hurricane. Tom said that he did not believe God caused this hurricane; "but," he said, "nothing, not even Katrina, not even our death, is beyond the redemptive grace of God; and in that sense God is sovereign. All the evil we see in the world would seem to bear witness that God is not powerful, but the doctrine of sovereignty says that God is more powerful than these signs of evil and that God will ultimately fold these into his purposes. Whether we're talking about natural disaster or the terrible things we do to one another, God will not let evil and destruction be the last word."

Many non-Calvinists struggle with the way in which pre-destination and divine sovereignty are described in Calvin's work and the work of those who came after him. But Tom Are's interpretation of these forces is one on which both Calvinists and non-Calvinists would be likely to agree.

Responding to God's Sovereignty

Let's look at how our Presbyterian friends' emphasis on the sovereignty of God can help us be more-authentically Christian.

When I think of the sovereignty of God, I think of God's ultimate reign over the cosmos—that he does have "the whole world in his hands." I know that one day this world will end; there will be a new heaven and a new earth, and the kingdom of God will consume the kingdoms of this world. This brings me great comfort. I know that an asteroid headed straight toward our planet, a terrible bio-disaster that wiped out all of humankind, or a global nuclear war that signaled our destruction could not overrule God's plan.

In my own life, I have tried to surrender to God's will. I long to be used by God, to bring glory to him, and one day to be with him in heaven. Because God is sovereign in my life, I am committed to serving him, come what may. I do not believe God makes us ill, but I may very well become seriously ill nonetheless. In my illness or health, in my poverty or wealth, I belong to God. If I am to die tomorrow, or forty years from now, I will never be outside of God's grasp. I know that he is always with me, and knowing that brings me great peace.

This belief mirrors what the psalmist was saying in Psalm 139. Ponder again these words:

> In your book were written
> all the days that were formed for me,
> when none of them as yet existed.
> How weighty to me are your thoughts, O God!
> How vast is the sum of them!
> I try to count them—they are more than the sand;
> I come to the end—I am still with you.
>   (Psalm 139:16b-18)

It is also the message of Job, who faced the most terrible of life's circumstances, not because he was evil and God was punishing him, but for reasons that even the Book of Job does not fully disclose. In Chapter 13, Job's friends have begged him simply to curse God, admit he is a sinner, and die. Instead he says, "Though he slay me, yet will I hope in him" (Job 13:15; NIV). Job is saying that no matter what happens, he will continue to trust in God. In Job 19:25-27a, after losing his home, property, and children, Job speaks these words of trust in the sovereignty and ultimate triumph of God:

> For I know that my Redeemer lives,
> and that at the last he will stand upon the earth;
> and after my skin has been thus destroyed,

then in my flesh I shall see God,
whom I shall see on my side,
and my eyes shall behold, and not another.
(Job 19:25-27*a*)

This statement reflects an absolute trust that God rules over everything, even death.

I also believe the sovereignty of God has to do with God's work in our daily lives. I try to wake up every day seeking to serve my Sovereign, to live according to his precepts, and to follow his will. I believe God is at work in our lives, not by micromanaging or moving us as pawns on a chessboard, but by seeking to influence us and to lead us according to his will. Our task is to listen and to follow. When we do that, we will often find ourselves experiencing "God incidents," situations that might seem like coincidences to some but in which we can see God's purposes and plans unfolding. I am convinced these happen all the time, but often we miss them.

I will offer just one example of "God incidents" that happen every day, if we are only watching for them. Recently my wife and daughters were out of town and I was alone. I decided to eat supper at one of my favorite restaurants, taking my computer and books so I could read and work while enjoying a leisurely meal. As I was finishing, a woman who attends the Church of the Resurrection stopped by my table and said, "I'm here with a friend who is in real trouble right now. I don't want to bother you, but I wonder if you could help me decide what I might say to her." I paid for my supper and stopped by to see her friend. We talked for a little while about the friend's life situation and prayed together as we sat in the restaurant. I believe we all felt that God was at work in that moment. Did God make each of us show up in that restaurant at just that time? I do not think so. But it is possible that God was influencing us, and we happened to have followed his influence. My decision to eat at that particular restaurant, my parishioner's feeling that she should come to my table and speak to me, and my sense that I needed to stop and talk with her friend—in all these events God's Spirit may have been at work. They could have been a coincidence; but, experiencing enough such events on a regular basis, I have come to believe that God regularly works in these ways if only we are listening and looking for them.

All of which takes me back to the issue of hurricanes and other natural disasters. In 2005 we all watched in shock and disbelief as Katrina devastated the people and cities along the Gulf Coast in Mississippi and Louisiana. Flooding overwhelmed a major American city. There were over 400,000 refugees here in the United States and 170,000 children with nowhere to go to school. People slept on the highway, going without food or water for days; and in some cases the dead lay unattended. I do not believe God brought about Hurricane Katrina to teach, to punish, or to pursue his purposes. Hurricanes are naturally occurring events, which happen with some regularity. We may even discover that human beings could be exacerbating the situation, either by where we build cities or through the production of greenhouse gas emissions. When human beings come in conflict with the forces of nature that we cannot control, these forces are bound, at times, to bring devastation and destruction.

I believe God designed a world in which all these forces work together to maintain an equilibrium that has made human existence possible. The question is not why God brought Hurricane Katrina to bear on the Gulf Coast, but, in a world where hurricanes will occasionally bring destruction, what response the Sovereign of the Universe, our King, wishes us to make. I believe God calls us to show compassion, to reach out as his hands and voice, and to serve him by serving those in need. We are compelled by him to surround with love and care those who struggle. In this way God uses people as his agents to accomplish his work of sustaining and caring for his creation.

In the end I am grateful for our Presbyterian friends and their reminder that God rules, that we are his subjects, and that our task is always to be ready to pursue his will.

1. From Hartford Institute for Religion Research at www.hirr.hartsem.edu/cong/nondenom.html.

CHAPTER 5

ANGLICANISM: COMMON PRAYER

Seven times a day I praise you
for your righteous ordinances.
(Psalm 119:164)

But now more than ever the word about Jesus spread
abroad; many crowds would gather to hear him and to be
cured of their diseases. But he would withdraw to deserted
places and pray.
(Luke 5:15-16)

Rejoice always, pray without ceasing, give thanks in all cir-
cumstances; for this is the will of God in Christ Jesus for you.
(1 Thessalonians 5:16-18)

A Brief History of the English Reformation

Christianity's sixteenth-century reform movements—first
Luther's and then Calvin's—swept across the continent of
Europe like wildfire. In a short time nearly half of Europe had
separated from the Roman Catholic Church to form their own
churches, predominantly Lutheran or Reformed. Germany,
Sweden, Denmark, and Norway tended to follow Luther.

Switzerland and France followed Calvin. Italy, Spain, and portions of France and Germany remained Roman Catholic. But it was the Reformation as it took place in England that would profoundly shape American religion in the years to come.

As on the continent, the Catholic Church in England had lost its vitality. Kenneth Scott Latourette, in his classic study *A History of Christianity,* writes, "Fifteenth-century English Christianity had in it much of corruption and decay. Many of the devout were saying that the monasteries had outlived their usefulness and that the monks were idle and ignorant. Hundreds of the clergy had concubines."[1]

Latourette goes on to note that the British monarchs were increasingly resentful of the outside influence of the pope in their internal affairs. Long before King Henry VIII formally removed the Church of England from the pope's control, men like John Wycliffe and William Tyndale were calling for the reform of the church. Wycliffe, a Catholic priest, was raising questions regarding Catholic doctrine and encouraging the reading of the Bible in the language of the people 150 years before Luther's protest.

While earnest people of faith were calling for reform in the Catholic Church in England, it was a king's desire for an heir that ultimately led the English church to split from the Roman Catholic Church and become the Church of England.

You may recall the story, which began with King Henry VIII. At the age of eighteen Henry married his brother's widow, Katharine of Aragon. She had multiple miscarriages and one son, Henry, who lived for two months; but Katharine produced no male offspring who survived. (She did have one daughter, Mary, who survived and later became queen; but we are getting ahead of our story.) Katharine's difficulty in producing a male heir, coupled with Henry's romantic interest in Anne Boleyn, led him to seek an annulment of his marriage, which the pope refused to grant. In 1533, Henry married Anne Boleyn without the pope's annulment of his previous marriage. The pope responded by excommunicating him. King Henry and the British Parliament in turn removed the Church of England from the pope's control and declared that King Henry VIII was "the only Supreme Head in Earth of the Church of England."

It is important to note that King Henry did not intend to change any of the church's doctrines or practices, except to wrest oversight of the church from Rome. He understood the Church of England to be the *Catholic* Church of England. During his reign, a few Lutherans and other Protestants were even put to death, including William Tyndale. Nevertheless, the reading of the Bible in English was allowed and came to be encouraged. Henry died in 1547; and his sickly son, Edward VI, succeeded him. (Edward's mother was Jane Seymour, Henry's third wife, who died shortly after Edward was born.) Edward was only nine when he came to the throne, and he died at the age of sixteen; but during his short reign, influential Protestants—predominantly Calvinists—came to England, spurring reforms in the Church of England. Clergy were allowed to marry; and the first Book of Common Prayer, a book in the language of the people for daily prayers and worship, was prepared.

After Edward's brief reign, his older half-sister Mary came to power. Unlike Edward, who was Protestant, Mary held strong Catholic convictions. During her five-year reign, she sought to turn back the Protestant reforms and bring the Church of England back under Roman authority. Married clergy were relieved of their duties, and some of the leading reformers were arrested and either beheaded or burned at the stake. It was this persecution that led some to call her "Bloody Mary."

The *Via Media* of Anglicanism

In twenty-five years, England had gone from being Roman Catholic to English Catholic to Calvinistic Protestant and back to Roman Catholic. The situation could have led to chaos had it not been for the strong and wise leadership of Queen Elizabeth I, the half-sister of Mary and Edward, who came to the throne in 1558 and reigned for forty-five years. It was she who negotiated what is known as the Elizabethan Settlement, and her approach to religion helped to shape the Anglican Church down to the present time. With large numbers of both Catholics and Protestants in the population, Elizabeth tried to forge, in the national church, what we know as a *via media*: a middle way. The church aimed to draw from both Catholic and Protestant traditions, never returning to Catholicism, but not fully embracing Luther or Calvin either.

After Elizabeth's reign, King James I came to power. He had a measure of disdain for both Catholicism and the kind of Calvinistic Puritanism that was taking root in England. Noting that the most-popular English Bible, the Geneva Bible, was strongly influenced by Calvin's thought, he authorized a new translation of the Bible that would navigate the *via media* between Catholicism and Calvinism. This Bible was finally published in 1611 and is known as the King James Version.

This idea of the *via media* has long been associated with Anglicans and, as they are known in America, Episcopalians. The Very Reverend Terry White, Dean of the Cathedral at Grace and Holy Trinity Church in Kansas City, Missouri, points out the practical realities of the phrase:

Historically, *via media* has referred to a middle way between Protestantism and Roman Catholicism in the West. Marks of the Anglican Church that are very much a part of Catholic teaching and heritage would be the three-fold ministry of bishop, priest, and deacon; the seven sacraments that are celebrated, with particular emphasis on Holy Baptism and on Holy Eucharist; the sense of reverence in liturgy; and reliance upon the spiritual disciplines that have existed in the church for centuries. The more reformed or Protestant elements of our tradition include the fact that bishops, priests, and deacons can be married; and that in most parts of the communion, including the United States, they can be women; and that laity share very much in the ministry of the church, since baptism makes everyone a minister of the gospel.

We have seen how Presbyterians understand church history:

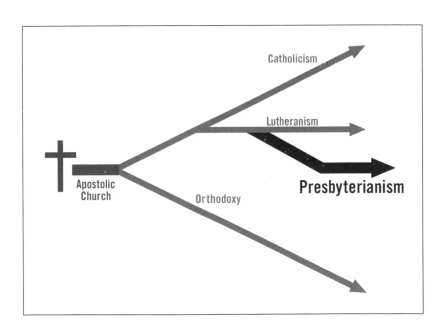

The early Presbyterians believed that Luther had not gone far enough in his reforms, so they sought to take the church a bit farther from Catholicism. But Anglicans believed that Luther and Calvin had gone a bit too far and sought to navigate a middle path between Catholics and Protestants. This chart shows church history from an Anglican or Episcopalian perspective:

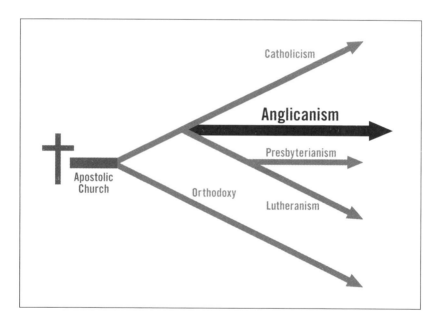

Anglicans speak of a three-legged stool by which they determine what they believe and practice as Christians: Scripture, tradition, and reason. Scripture is the first and most-important leg. The second leg is tradition: how Christians have understood their faith through the centuries. The third leg is reason, as applied to the other two.

Episcopal worship looks more Catholic than that of other Protestant churches. Episcopalians note that, like Roman

Catholic and Orthodox Christians, they worship with all their senses. They use their bodies to bow and to cross themselves, they listen to words and music, they smell the incense, they see the light of candles, and they taste the bread and wine of the Eucharist. The Episcopal Church embraces a view of Holy Communion which, while not identical to the Roman Catholic view, is very close to it. Episcopalians believe in two Gospel sacraments (Holy Communion and baptism) but view the other five Roman Catholic sacraments as "sacramental rites." The Episcopal Church allows clergy to marry, emphasizes the priesthood of all believers, and looks to the Scriptures as its primary basis for faith and practice.

Lex Orandi, Lex Credendi

Prayer is a key part of any discussion of the Episcopal Church, which is known for its Book of Common Prayer. Jesus said that God is looking for people who will worship him in spirit and in truth; who will love God with all their heart, soul, mind, and strength; and who will then live that love toward their neighbors. And while there are a variety ways in which we come to know God and grow in our love for him, central to that quest are prayer, praise, and worship. Without prayer, we simply cannot continue to live as God desires. As we pray, so we believe; and if we truly believe, we must pray.

That brings us to the Latin phrase *lex orandi, lex credendi,* which contains an idea important to Episcopalians. It means literally, "The law of prayer is the law of belief"; and it is understood by many to mean that praying and worshiping are the most-important things we do. The essence of the Christian faith is found in worshiping together, in spending daily time in prayer, and in listening for God's voice. These practices should shape the faith we confess, and the Episcopal Church takes them very seriously.

"Our emphasis on the Book of Common Prayer," says the Very Reverend White, "has encouraged all members of the church to be regular in their prayer life. The present version for the American church contains several 'offices,' morning and evening prayer, as well as noonday prayer and the office of compline, which would be said just before going to bed. There is a daily two-year lectionary that takes people through the Psalms and various lessons of both Testaments. There are also corporate prayers. The Episcopal Church is not a confessional church; we don't have a long confession of faith written out or a *Summa Theologica* containing all the teachings of the Church. What we have is the Book of Common Prayer."

Notice the Scripture passages that opened this chapter. From Luke's Gospel we see Jesus' own practices of prayer. Jesus had been ministering to the crowds—healing the sick, preaching the good news, touching people. But notice Luke 5:16. The Scripture says that Jesus "would withdraw to deserted places and pray." Again and again we find this in the Gospels. Before he selected his disciples, after he had fed the multitudes, as he was preparing for his crucifixion, as he hung on the cross— Jesus prayed.

Why did he do this? Jesus did this because prayer allowed him to focus on and hear from the Father; to experience his presence; and to find comfort, peace, and strength. Jesus needed to do this. His capacity to minister and his ability to face challenges depended on prayer.

Paul, through his epistles, repeatedly tells us of his own prayers and then commands us to pray. He says in Philippians 4:6-7, "Do not worry about anything, but in everything by prayer and supplication with thanksgiving let your requests be made known to God. And the peace of God, which surpasses all understanding, will guard your hearts and your minds in Christ Jesus." I cannot think of these verses without being reminded of the stanza of that old gospel song which says,

> O what peace we often forfeit,
> O what needless pain we bear,
> all because we do not carry
> everything to God in prayer."[2]

I recall speaking with a couple who were in the midst of marital difficulties. They previously had been active at the Church of the Resurrection but had relocated to another city. I asked about their worship attendance and learned that they had not been active in church since moving away. I asked about their prayer life, which they indicated was virtually non-existent. Of course they were struggling! It is prayer and worship that keep us centered, fill us with strength, help us know God's will, and give us the grace to pursue it.

The Book of Common Prayer reminds us of the importance of prayer, worship, and discipline in our lives. We can know all the theology in the world; but if we are not spending time in communion with God, it will all be for naught. As with the Catholic tradition of the Benedictines, Episcopalians invite us to consider setting aside certain times of the day to commune with God through prayer, worship, and reading the Psalms.

Episcopalians also invite us to "pray the hours"—at least two or three set times or offices of prayer every day. The pattern is to begin each day in prayer and reading the Psalms. The morning daily office is called "lauds," which means praise. When you awaken, you pause to praise God and place your life in his hands, to invite him to guide, lead, use, and walk with you throughout the day. At noon you pause in the middle of your day for what is known as "sext," named for the sixth hour of the day. Here you reset your spiritual compass. You pause to pray, to give thanks for the morning, and to ask for grace for the afternoon; and you read another psalm. Then at sunset you observe another time of prayer and worship, called "vespers." The final time of prayer for the day is "compline," which comes from the Latin for "to complete," since this time of prayer completes the day. At this time you pause to thank God for the day and examine what you have done, inviting God to help you see where you sinned or fell short of his plans and to teach you how to live more according to his will the following day. Once again you read a psalm.

Episcopalians invite us to take seriously the idea that saying we believe something is not enough. Our prayers and praise and worship are what shape belief, and true belief will manifest itself in these acts. They call us to bring discipline and order to our prayer lives. They invite us to have multiple times of prayer and praise and worship each day; at least two or three are suggested as a minimum. They maintain that doing this really does make all the difference. Through prayer, Jesus found strength. Through prayer, we find the peace that passes understanding. And in prayer, rejoicing always, giving thanks in all circumstances, we discover the will of God in Christ Jesus for us.

1. From *A History of Christianity,* by Kenneth Scott Latourette (Prince Press, 1975); Volume II, page 797.

2. From "What a Friend We Have in Jesus," in *The United Methodist Hymnal* (Copyright © 1989 by The United Methodist Publishing House); 526.

CHAPTER 6

BAPTISTS:
BAPTISM, CONVERSION,
AND SCRIPTURE

For God so loved the world that he gave his only Son, so that everyone who believes in him may not perish but may have eternal life.

(John 3:16)

For the wages of sin is death, but the free gift of God is eternal life in Christ Jesus our Lord.

(Romans 6:23)

The Origin of the Baptists

In the English Reformation, Christians tried to navigate a middle way between Catholics and Calvin's Protestants, combining elements of each. To this day, the Anglican Church, or Episcopal Church as it is known in America, reflects this character and faith. In the 1600s in England, though, there were many among the clergy and laity who were dissatisfied with this middle path. They sought to purge the church of its Catholic or "high church" elements; to restore it to what they believed was its New Testament character; and to purify the church and its members, challenging them to lead a holy life. This group became known, initially in a derogatory way, as

"Puritans"; for their emphasis was on moral and spiritual purity. The Puritans were also known as Dissenters and Nonconformists. Many remained part of the Church of England, seeking to work for change from within; but the more-radical Puritans left the church, and among these were the Pilgrims. Another group of Puritans who called for more-radical reform and eventually left the church were the Baptists. Although some Baptists trace their faith to nonconformists throughout church history, the first Baptists as we know them came from the Puritan tradition in the Church of England.

Among Baptists' "radical" ideas was that baptism was only for adults; therefore, any Christian who was baptized as a child needed to be rebaptized. Every branch of Christianity we have studied so far (the Orthodox, the Catholics, the Lutherans, the Presbyterians, and the Anglicans) practiced infant baptism. But the Baptists held that only those practices explicitly described in the New Testament were to be made normative for the church. Since the New Testament only reports the baptism of adult converts who were called to repent and be baptized, it was reasoned that adult baptism was the only valid form of baptism. (Those who practice infant baptism point to circumcision as the precursor to infant baptism and see baptism as the outward sign of God's covenant with the people. They also see the stories of Lydia's household and the Philippian jailer's household being baptized in Acts 16 as possible examples of parents having their children baptized in the early church.) Since infants were not mature enough to understand what it meant to repent or be baptized, the practice of infant baptism was to be eliminated. The name "Baptist" was, in fact, originally a shortened version of Anapedobaptist, a mouthful of a term that refers to those against the baptism of infants. John Smyth, the first Baptist pastor we know of, rebaptized his entire congregation one Sunday. Interestingly enough, the early

Baptists did not baptize by immersion or even by sprinkling but by a practice called *affusion*, pouring water over the believer three times, in the name of the Father, Son, and Holy Spirit.

Although early Baptists shared a belief in adult baptism, they actually were made up of two distinct groups: General Baptists and Particular Baptists. General Baptists believed in general atonement—that is, that Christ died to save all who would repent. This was the group initially led by John Smyth in Amsterdam. Particular Baptists, who got their start in London, believed that Christ died only for a particular group, the elect. Theological diversity has continued, within the Baptist churches, to the present day.

Baptist Reforms

Baptists, in their call for more-radical reform, rejected not only infant baptism but also the liturgical elements of worship, the formal acts of worship, the vestments or dress of the clergy, and any other elements deemed to be Catholic. There was no processional; there were no acolytes and cross bearers, no candles. The early Baptists discarded symbolic acts and gestures. They also eliminated the altar, which was a place of sacrifice. Catholics spoke of the sacrifice of the Mass and the offering of the Eucharist as a way of re-presenting Jesus' sacrifice for us. Baptists, who rejected this view of the Eucharist, eliminated the altar entirely. Communion was deemed to be an act of remembrance, a memorial rather than a sacrament by which God conveys his grace; and it was observed far less frequently than in the sacramental churches. Instead of people coming forward for the Eucharist to receive Christ, they were invited forward to confess publicly their need for Christ and to invite him to forgive their sins and become Lord of their lives. The process also led most Baptist churches to drop the saying of the Lord's Prayer during worship, since they regarded it as an example of the vain repetition of words and as something that smacked of Catholicism. Baptist churches would not typically observe Ash Wednesday, Lent, or Advent, though in our time some have begun to explore these ancient holy days and seasons.

Because the Baptists were seen as radical even by many of the Puritans, they experienced persecution at times from both the high-church Anglicans and the low-church Puritans. This was true in America as well, which is why Baptists have traditionally been strong supporters of the separation of church and state, so that no one faith group's perspectives are supported by the state to the exclusion of others.

In line with our earlier looks at how various denominations see church history and their place in it, here is how Baptists might conceive it:

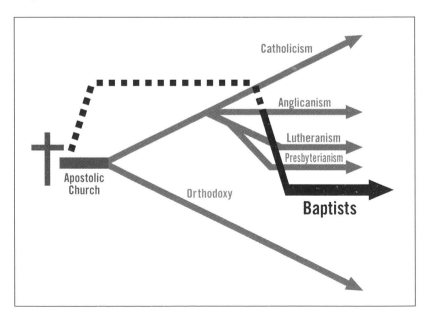

A solid line traces the roots of the Baptist traditions to the Anglican Church and shows that Baptists felt neither the Anglicans, the Lutherans, nor the Presbyterians had gone far enough in reforming the church. They proposed more-radical reforms. You will also notice the dotted line; many Baptists do not acknowledge their lineage through Catholicism and Anglicanism but see themselves as simply restoring the church to its earliest days. Baptists, as do Orthodox, Catholic, and most other Christian groups, believe their tradition is the most faithful to the New Testament message that can be found.

Baptist Beliefs and Practices

"Baptist" is a term that applies to a very broad family of Christians. There are about forty-five million Baptists of various types around the world, with thirty-three million living in the United States. Baptists traditionally have treasured the autonomy of the local congregation, and Baptist churches do not answer to bishops or to any outside authority. They do affiliate with like-minded Baptists in what are called "conventions."

Theologically, Baptist churches run the gamut from liberal to fundamentalist. The American Baptists tend to be the most moderate and are actually very close to United Methodists and Presbyterians in many ways. The largest group of Baptists is represented by the Southern Baptist Convention; but there are hundreds of other Baptist groups, including some who refuse to recognize the other Baptists as Christians. In part, diversity comes from the Baptist emphasis on the individual's own conscience and liberty when it comes to interpreting the Bible. Since it is difficult to find any two Christians who interpret the entire Bible in exactly the same way, divisions naturally arise in churches; and because of the historic emphasis on purity of doctrine within the Baptist churches, there is, among some, less tolerance for diverse interpretations. This tends to foster a need for some to form their own church when there is a disagreement within a particular congregation over biblical interpretation.

In spite of the diversity among Baptists, they do share some basic beliefs and practices. Baptists begin with the idea of a believers' church, the idea that the church is composed, not of those baptized as infants, but of those who have made a confession of faith in Christ. All church members must testify to a work of grace, with baptism viewed as its outward sign. Baptism, therefore, follows confession of faith. Although the practice of affusion was followed initially, as noted previously, Baptists began practicing baptism by immersion by 1641; and it has remained the normative mode to this day.

Believers' church, for the Baptists, includes a congregational church government, in which clergy and laity work together in the governance of the church. Two types of church officer are recognized: pastors and deacons.

Religious liberty is at the heart of Baptist identity. Faith is uncoerced, meaning that God alone is the judge of conscience, not the state or the religious establishment. Baptists believe that if conscience is essential to faith, then dissent is essential in the state. Dissent is seen as essential in the church as well, not just for individuals, but for congregations, resulting in the congregational autonomy that Baptists value so highly.

"The fact that Baptists come from this nonconformist background and that we don't have that governing body is a two-edged sword," says Dr. Jeff Adams, pastor of Kansas City Baptist Temple in Raytown, Missouri, an Independent Baptist congregation. "When we get mad at each other and have differing viewpoints, it's very tempting simply to branch off and form a new group. As a result, there's an absolute galaxy of Baptist groups.

"I will say this about most Southern Baptists," adds Dr. Adams. "They tend to be fundamental in their theology, but not necessarily fundamental in their attitudes. Sometimes I jokingly say to people, 'I'm an Independent Baptist, but I'm not mad about it!' Most Independent Baptists tend to be even more fundamentalist in attitude and doctrine than many of the Southern Baptists."

While Baptists do not use the creeds, they do have faith statements that are generally agreed upon by those who associate with a given convention. For Southern Baptists, this statement is called "The Baptist Faith and Message." There is much in that statement that other Protestants would agree with and a few things we would disagree with. Generally, our disagreements spring from how we view the Bible. Protestants look to the Bible as their primary guide to faith and practice. They typically speak of it as "inspired by God." But Protestants differ as to exactly how to understand the Bible's inspiration and, in turn, how to interpret the Bible appropriately. Southern Baptists, the largest of the Baptist churches, note that the Bible contains truth "without any mixture of error . . . therefore, all Scripture is totally true and trustworthy."[1] This view of Scripture is sometimes called "inerrancy." It is often coupled with a view of inspiration called "verbal, plenary inspiration," a phrase which means that every word in the Bible was inspired by God.

Many contemporary Baptists believe that the Bible must be seen as the first and ultimate source of truth regarding anything that it touches upon, whether it be science, history, or mathematics. For instance, if the Bible appears to be at odds with prevailing scientific theories, the theories must be wrong because the Bible is "totally true and trustworthy." Not all

Baptists would hold such views of Scripture, though many do. By contrast, the statements of faith by churches like The United Methodist Church do not make claims about the Bible's accuracy in matters of history or science, assuming that the biblical authors wrote in the light of the prevailing scientific knowledge and with the historical information they had access to at the time in which they wrote. Instead it is simply noted that the Bible "containeth all things necessary to salvation."[2]

In general, Baptists hold to the essentials of the faith as described in both the Apostles' Creed and the Nicene Creed, though they do not make use of those creeds. They also hold to the Protestant emphases of justification by faith and *sola scriptura* and *sola gratia*—Scripture alone and grace alone.

"Baptists believe, first and foremost," says Dr. Adams, "in the inspiration, infallibility, and preservation of Scripture. As a whole, they have been committed to the Word of God rather than to tradition and heritage; and that has been a core belief through the years. People from Baptist backgrounds have always placed a strong emphasis upon one's personal relationship with God, so that regenerate church membership was very important. Another great emphasis of Baptists traditionally has been on salvation by grace through faith alone —plus nothing, minus nothing. Those characteristics, along with the reservation of baptism for those who have already placed their faith in Christ—so that infants are not qualified—are some of the hallmarks of Baptists of just about any variety."

What Baptists Teach Us

I was reminded of the story of the Baptist and United Methodist pastors who were walking down the street together when it started to rain. The United Methodist just sauntered along, enjoying the gentle autumn shower; but the Baptist hurried to get out of the rain. When the United Methodist caught up, he said, "You're a Baptist; tell me you're not afraid of a little rain!" To which the Baptist replied, "I'm not afraid of the water. I just prefer not to be sprinkled on!"

While other Protestants often baptize by sprinkling and Baptists do so by immersion, there is much we agree upon. I would lift up three qualities I appreciate in Baptists that I hope will shape your faith.

Bible Study and a Love of the Word

The first quality I love about Baptists is their love of the Bible and Bible study. Seeking to live according to the Bible, loving to read it, and striving to follow it—these are things Baptists have traditionally stood for. These are, by the way, things that other Christian groups have traditionally stood for as well. For example, the founder of Methodism, John Wesley, said he was *homo unius libri,* a man of one book. United Methodists and more-conservative Baptists may differ in how they read this book—with Baptists taking it word for word and seeking to apply it literally to their lives and Methodists (along with more-moderate Baptists) listening for God's word as it speaks through the words of the human authors; asking questions of the text; and interpreting it with the help of tradition, reason, and experience. But despite these differences we both love the Scriptures and believe they are inspired by God. If you are not a Bible reader and have not been in Bible study, I would take this opportunity to say that you are missing out on a profound experience that will change your life; and I hope that you will come to read and love the Scriptures.

A Zeal for Missions and Evangelism

A second quality I love about most Baptists is their passion for inviting people to come to Christ, expressed both in their personal lives and in their churches' support for start-ing new churches and sending out missionaries from their congregations. Baptists have the profound conviction that people who do not know Christ are lost and that our job as Christians and as churches is to seek and save the lost. It is with this sense of conviction that some members of Baptist Temple in the Kansas City area have left their corporate jobs and gone to live overseas in order to start churches and schools and thereby help others know Christ. It is this con-viction that has led them to have members of their church leave with a pastor to go start a new congregation that will reach a new population for Christ.

"In the last fifteen years," Dr. Adams notes, "we have trained, commissioned, and sent out of this church directly some seventy-three of our own members to be missionaries, not only in this country, but in other countries around the world." Baptist Temple members have also helped to launch a dozen churches around the Kansas City area.

I pray that you might catch the spirit of Baptist Temple in your church, loving people around the world who are lost and desiring to help them come to faith in Christ to such an extent that you and others in your congregation might become modern-day missionaries and apostles for Christ.

The Simple Salvation Message

The last quality I love about Baptists is something that mainline churches often have neglected in the last hundred years: an emphasis on the simple salvation message of the gospel. In our sophistication, in stressing the social gospel and social action, we sometimes forget that the Christian life begins with a personal decision to follow Christ. We some-times lose sight of why people need Jesus Christ, of why *we* need Jesus Christ. I would like to take a moment to remind you of the simple gospel as it is preached in many Baptist churches.

The gospel begins with the recognition of a problem. That problem is sin. The Bible tells the story of the origin of human sin by speaking of Adam and Eve, who disobeyed God and ate of the forbidden fruit, thus bringing an end to innocence, an awareness of guilt, and a separation from God. We have been struggling with sin ever since.

It has been said that Billy Graham, like other famous evangelists before him, was known for preaching with the Bible in one hand and the newspaper in the other. Dr. Graham has done this, in part, because the newspaper is filled with examples of human brokenness in the midst of human attempts at doing good. As I wrote this book, the news media offered reports on a charity that was said to be supporting terrorism and on the arrest of several prominent people for public intoxication. There was also coverage of a rock star hospitalized for drug addiction, a journalist fired for making misleading statements, and a man found guilty of murdering several hunters—and all this was just on the first two pages of a single edition of the daily newspaper.

We all see the evidence of sin in our life, if we are honest with ourselves. Sin comes in the form of pride and self-centeredness, little white lies, materialism, gossip and backbiting, hardened hearts, thoughtlessness, infidelity, lack of patience. Have I named your sin yet? The fact that we throw away food while thirty thousand people die from starvation every day, that we consume an inordinate amount of the world's resources while others live at subpoverty levels, that at times what serves America's foreign policy interests actually hurts the interests of other nations—all these actions are only symptoms of the greater problem: a sickness of the soul that separates us from others and from God.

In Romans 6:23 the apostle Paul tells us that the wages, or the end result, of sin is death: eternal separation from God. But the gospel is good news because God offers a remedy for sin. That is where John 3:16 comes in. Recently, I was speaking to a man who said, "I was told that if you took all the Bible away except for the Book of John, you'd still have enough to find salvation. And if you took away all the chapters of John but the third chapter, you would still have enough to find salvation. And if you took away all the verses of the third chapter of John except the sixteenth, you would still have enough there to find salvation."

John 3:16 says that "God so loved the world...." This is a profound statement. God loves the world. God loves people. God loves. It is out of this love that God acts. He sent Jesus, his only begotten Son, to walk among us to teach us about God and what it means to be truly human, to give us hope, and to call us to repentance. Ultimately, Jesus died at the hands of people who were the religious leaders of his time. He died on the cross, and his death there was used by God as the means of remedying the spiritual consequences of human sin. Baptists emphasize the substitutionary theory of atonement, which says that Jesus died in our place. Being God himself, he took for himself the punishment that we deserve—death—and he satisfied the requirements of justice. Sin must be punished, and Jesus endured the punishment of sin on our behalf.

There are a host of theories to explain how this works. Most Baptists simply accept this truth: It was God's plan that Jesus' death would be the means for delivering us from the consequences of our sin, and in this way he offers us forgiveness and makes available to us everlasting life. Thus, "God so loved the world that he gave his only Son, so that everyone who believes in him may not perish but may have eternal life" (John 3:16).

To receive this gift of forgiveness, of right standing with God and of eternal life, we do not have to do anything except accept the gift—trust in it, trust in him. The apostle Paul said that "if you confess with your lips that Jesus is Lord and believe in your heart that God raised him from the dead, you will be saved" (Romans 10:9). He said that once we do that, we are new; the Holy Spirit begins to work in us to change us from the inside out. And we live in the hope of everlasting life.

We can live out the rest of our days carrying our sin with us. We can try our best to overcome it. We can live separated from God, without his grace and mercy. Or we can accept his forgiveness and welcome Christ as our Savior, gaining the knowledge of grace, the power of the Holy Spirit, a new sense of purpose, and the promise of everlasting life. But we must, at some point, make this decision; we must claim Christ. The Scripture says that he stands at the door and knocks (Revelation 3:20), but he will not force himself on us. He awaits our willingness to invite him in.

Pastors deal with lost and dying people on a regular basis. One of the pastors on the staff of my church was recently ministering with someone who was in a situation of total and complete lostness, one that seemed to be overwhelming. In the midst of this person's lostness, the pastor said to her, "When we are utterly lost, we might finally understand how much we need a Savior." To which the individual replied, *"I need a Savior."* Perhaps you feel this way now.

Recently, Tom, one of my parishioners, passed away. Tom enjoyed life, but he knew it would not last forever. He was in worship every Sunday when he was not sick and some Sundays when he was. I would see him at the 7:45 AM service sitting next to his wife, Patty, and could tell that he was not well; but I could also see that he was not willing to be anywhere else. He knew that when this life is over, we have a building not made by human hands that is eternal in the heavens (See Hebrews 9:24.). One Tuesday morning, Patty, his family, and I gathered around Tom's bed and prayed for him one last time; and we did so as people who knew that Tom was safe in the arms of the Good Shepherd. There was comfort and even joy that came from knowing that Tom belonged to Jesus Christ and that he had trusted Christ as his Savior. When Tom passed, we grieved as those who have hope.

So here is my question for you: Are you able yet to understand that you need what Jesus offers? Do you recognize that you cannot save yourself? Would you be willing to embrace his love and allow him to embrace you? Perhaps you have been a lifelong churchgoer, but you have never actually asked Jesus Christ to be your Savior. Maybe you are now ready to commit or recommit your life to Christ.

In the Baptist tradition people are invited to come forward, to express by the act of getting out of their seats and walking to the front of the church that they have chosen to follow Christ, to pray with one another, and in this way to make a commitment to Christ. As they do so, the prayer offered is often something like this one, which I think is an appropriate conclusion to our look at the Baptist tradition. I invite you to make this your prayer:

> Lord Jesus, I need you. I accept you as my Savior. Forgive my sins. Wash me clean, and make me new. I choose to follow you as my Lord. Help me to live according to your will each day. I wish to be your disciple. Teach me your ways. I offer my heart and life to you. Use me as you will. I pray this in your name and for your sake, Jesus. Amen.

1. From "The Baptist Faith and Message"; See www.sbc.net/bfm/bfm2000.asp.
2. See Article V of the Articles of Religion at www.archives.umc.org/interior.asp?ptid=1&mid=1649.

CHAPTER 7

PENTECOSTALISM: THE POWER OF THE SPIRIT

I will pour out my Spirit on all flesh.
(Joel 2:28)

You will receive power when the Holy Spirit has come upon you; and you will be my witnesses in Jerusalem, in all Judea and Samaria, and to the ends of the earth.
(Acts 1:8)

When the day of Pentecost had come, they were all together in one place. And suddenly from heaven there came a sound like the rush of a violent wind, and it filled the entire house where they were sitting. Divided tongues, as of fire, appeared among them, and a tongue rested on each of them. All of them were filled with the Holy Spirit and began to speak in other languages, as the Spirit gave them ability.
(Acts 2:1-4)

What Is Pentecostalism?

We look now at the youngest of the major bodies in Christianity, the Pentecostal family of churches. Pentecostalism takes its name from the Jewish festival of Pentecost; it was at this festival around AD 30 that the Holy Spirit descended on the first Christians, and the church was born. Pentecostals are known for energetic and passion-filled worship and an emphasis on supernatural experiences of the Holy Spirit. Although the official beginning of Pentecostalism is usually set at 1901, its roots reach back another 200 years through John Wesley and the Methodist Church. So we will need to discuss a little Methodist history to set the stage for our study of Pentecostalism.

In the early 1700s, the Church of England offered worship that was beautiful but subdued, speaking perhaps more to the intellect than to the heart. Its dominant strain seemed to place little emphasis on holiness and seemed satisfied with a tepid kind of faith, at least from John Wesley's perspective. John and his brother Charles, both Anglican priests, began to seek more from their faith. They pursued rigorous spiritual disciplines of prayer, Bible study, and works of piety and met with others in small groups for accountability and growth in faith. In 1738, both Wesley brothers had profound experiences in which they came to have an assurance of their salvation. As a result, they incorporated into their beliefs the need for conversion and the continuing work of the Holy Spirit in the life of the believer, with the aim being sanctification; that is, removing the bent toward sin and shaping the Christian into one who loves God and neighbor. John Wesley went on to be a leader of the great eighteenth-century religious revival in England.

Wesley's followers, called Methodists, were known for their spiritual passion and for religious experiences that were sometimes deemed, by more traditional Anglicans, to be excessive. Wesley and his followers seemed able to hold together, sometimes in tension with one another, the intellect and the passions, the evangelical and the social gospels. But in nineteenth-century

America, the Methodist movement found itself divided between those who emphasized the heart (Christian experience, personal holiness, and the evangelistic gospel) and those who emphasized reason, intellect, and the social gospel. The former were known for their camp meetings, in which people on the frontiers would come together by wagon, pitch their tents, and hold revivals led by Methodist preachers. The latter became known for their Chautauquas, gatherings characterized not by emotional gospel preaching, but by lectures on the Bible, culture, and the social issues of the time.

During the nineteenth century, a number of groups broke away from the Methodist movement to form their own churches, nearly all emphasizing holiness or sanctification. They included the Nazarenes and their predecessors, the Church of God (Anderson, Indiana); the Adventists; the Salvation Army; the Wesleyan Church; and others. These groups tended to be more conservative theologically than the Methodists, and they placed a greater emphasis on both personal piety and personal fervor or experience.

Pentecostalism was born out of this holiness movement in 1901 at Bethel Bible College in Topeka, Kansas. Charles Fox Parham, who had a Methodist background, was teaching at Bethel. His study of the Book of Acts led him to wonder if the works of the Holy Spirit recorded there could not still happen in the church. Parham came to believe that what he called "baptism in the Holy Spirit" was separate from the believer's receipt of the Holy Spirit at salvation. He felt that such an experience—an immersion in the Holy Spirit—would be demonstrated first by speaking in tongues, whereby the Holy Spirit enabled Christians to speak in a language they had not previously known or to speak in a completely unintelligible language. Parham began to invite his students to receive this manifestation of the Holy Spirit, and it was in 1901 that a woman named Agnes Ozman had an experience such as Parham had described and began to speak in an unintelligible language. From there, the Pentecostal fire quickly spread to Los Angeles in 1906 and to Texas, Missouri, and a host of other places.

Modern-day Pentecostals view the experience of speaking in tongues as normative, believing that it is as available today as it was in the first century. Those in non-Pentecostal denominations who have had the Pentecostal experience of the Holy Spirit are typically called "Charismatics," from the Greek word used in the New Testament for spiritual gifts (*charismata*); and today it is estimated that there are as many as 600 million Christians worldwide who are either Pentecostal or Charistmatic.[1]

We have seen that most Christian denominations claim to preserve the earliest traditions of the church, some by way of continuity, others by a return to it. Baptists, we saw, view church history this way:

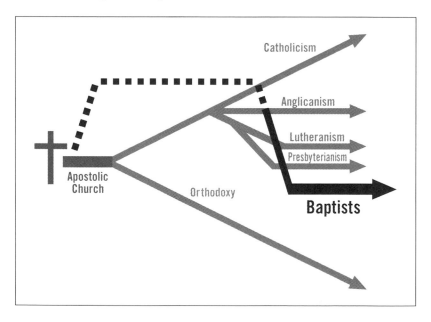

Pentecostals would say that Baptists have not gone back far enough to reclaim the practices of the New Testament sufficiently, for they have missed the pivotal experience of the apostolic church: the baptism of the Holy Spirit. As a result, this is how Pentecostals view church history and their role in it:

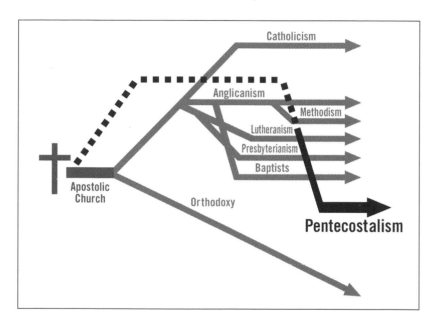

Four Major Emphases of Pentecostalism

So, what do Pentecostals believe? While they do not typically make use of the creeds, most Pentecostal groups would generally hold to the essentials of the faith as described in the Nicene Creed and Apostles' Creed. In addition, there are four major emphases in nearly all Pentecostal churches.

The Baptism of the Holy Spirit

The experience that sets one apart as a Pentecostal or Charismatic is the belief in and desire to experience the "baptism of the Holy Spirit." You will recall that John the Baptist began his public ministry saying, "I baptize you with water for repentance, but one who is more powerful than I is coming after me; I am not worthy to carry his sandals. He will baptize you with the Holy Spirit and fire" (Matthew 3:11). Most Christians believe the Holy Spirit baptizes or comes upon and covers us at our baptism or confirmation. Pentecostals would agree that the Spirit comes upon us when we commit our lives to Christ; but they believe that there is a subsequent experience, what is called a "second work of grace," at which time the Holy Spirit completely immerses believers, filling them with power.

"It's like taking a cup and pouring water into it," says the Reverend Dr. George Westlake, senior pastor of the Sheffield Assembly of God Church in Kansas City, Missouri. "The cup has water—that's salvation. You receive the Holy Spirit. But baptism of the Spirit is like taking that cup and putting it down in the water and bringing it up full and running over. In that experience you receive power to be a real witness for Jesus Christ. It doesn't make you any more spiritual than anybody else, but it gives you more power in your own life to be used by God in a very special way."

Jesus said in Acts 1:8, "You will receive power when the Holy Spirit has come upon you; and you will be my witnesses in Jerusalem, in all Judea and Samaria, and to the ends of the earth." Pentecostals believe that, as in the days of the Book of Acts, when believers are baptized in the Holy Spirit, they will speak in other languages or tongues. While on the Day of Pentecost the apostles spoke in existing languages that they had not known before, Pentecostals believe that most often those speaking in tongues speak in a language that is unintelligible to listeners, except to those who have a supernatural gift of interpretation.

Dr. Westlake can speak firsthand about this experience and what it means. Sheffield Assembly of God is one of the largest Pentecostal churches in the United States, averaging five thousand worshipers per weekend. Business leaders and prostitutes sit side by side in this racially diverse congregation, made up of people who have had or are seeking the kind of experience described by Pastor Westlake.

Speaking of his own experience of baptism in the Holy Spirit, Dr. Westlake told me, "I was in the prayer room at our home church. I was just praising the Lord and saying, 'God, I need power in my life'; and all of a sudden my tongue and my lips started doing different things, and a different language started coming out of my lips. This was something I could control. The Bible teaches us that we submit everything to the Holy Spirit, but he never takes control away; he never takes away your free will. Based on what happened to me, I can tell you that speaking in tongues is only the outward manifestation. The inward experience is even more powerful."

Pentecostals typically teach that the evidence that one has been baptized in the Holy Spirit is speaking in tongues, and it is here that non-Pentecostals would take the greatest exception to what the Pentecostals teach. Many non-Pentecostals, including most of the denominations we have studied so far, would allow that the Holy Spirit may give the gift of tongues; but they would also note that the gift, as first given on Pentecost, was the ability to speak a foreign language and that it was used by the Spirit for evangelizing Jews who spoke other languages and were present on the Day of Pentecost in Jerusalem. Non-Pentecostals would say that while tongues as described by Pentecostals may be a gift of the Holy Spirit, it is not the evidence of the baptism of the Holy Spirit. They would say that the evidence of the baptism or infilling of the Holy Spirit is the fruit of the Spirit, along with the strength, leadership, guidance, and presence of the Spirit in the life of the believer.

I came to faith in Christ in a Pentecostal church as a fourteen-year-old. After I made my decision to follow Christ, my pastor encouraged me to seek the "baptism of the Holy Ghost." After weeks and weeks of going to the altar at the conclusion of the church service with the other kids in the youth group, praying for this experience, I finally received this "baptism" in my bedroom one night as I was praying before going to sleep. As I was praying, I began to visualize certain words or syllables in my head, which I began to express in prayer. Unintelligible words began to form on my lips. In a sense, it was like praying without trying to limit the prayer to words and syntax.

I believe that my experience that night and my interpretation of that experience were shaped by what my church taught at the time. It was real, but it was not the life-changing experience some have described. I found praying in this way to be soothing at times. I did feel more open to the Spirit's power than I had before. But today I believe that the Holy Spirit had already filled me at my conversion and that my courage and boldness were tied to my daily inviting the Spirit to work in me, more than to the particular experience of speaking in an unintelligible tongue. This conclusion is perhaps part of the reason I am not a Pentecostal pastor today. I do not believe that speaking in tongues is the evidence of the baptism of the Spirit. At the same time, I do believe that all of us need and can be filled with the Holy Spirit and that the infilling of the Holy Spirit will give us power in our lives.

A Personal Relationship With Christ

A second major emphasis in Pentecostalism is having a personal relationship with Jesus Christ. While Pentecostals believe it is necessary for one to accept Christ as Savior and Lord, what is pivotal is having a personal relationship with Jesus Christ. All Christians believe that it is possible to speak to Christ, to listen for his voice, and to love him. Some Christians have a greater sense of this personal relationship than others. Some serve the Lord, seek the Lord, and strive to follow the Lord but never have strong feelings of closeness to him. Others, in every denomination, have a profound sense of their personal friendship and relationship with Christ. Pentecostals place a strong emphasis on the emotional dimensions of one's relationship with Jesus Christ.

The Second Coming of Christ

A third major emphasis of Pentecostals is the imminent return of Jesus Christ. Pentecostals recall the words of Joel 2:28, which says, "I will pour out my Spirit on all flesh." The experience that Charles Fox Parham and others had of being baptized by the Holy Spirit was seen as a direct fulfillment of this passage from Joel and a sure sign that the Second Coming was about to take place. This belief has been a hallmark of Pentecostal preaching ever since. Most Pentecostal pastors will not predict dates for the Lord's return, but for many years it was taught that the Lord would return before 1988—forty years after the reconstitution of the nation of Israel in 1948.

"I am a firm believer that Jesus Christ is coming back for his church," says Dr. Westlake. "He could come tonight. That's what really brought the Pentecostal power back at the turn of the century: People started preaching the fact that Jesus Christ could come back today. Now, he might not come back for twenty years because God's time isn't our time; and there's no such thing as time with God. But every prophecy has been fulfilled, so he really is coming. And the Bible said we are to live as men and women expecting our Lord."

Despite Dr. Westlake's cautionary words, there is a sense among many in the Pentecostal movement that the return of Jesus Christ will be within the lifetime of most of us living today. That sense is reflected in the great gospel songs frequently sung in the Pentecostal churches of the past, songs like "I'll Fly Away" and "Soon and Very Soon, We Are Going to See the King."

Modern-day Miracles and Healing

The final emphasis we will consider concerns modern-day miracles and healings. Oral Roberts was one of the best-known ambassadors for Pentecostalism until 1968 when, to everyone's surprise, he joined The United Methodist Church. He had taken his "canvas cathedral" across the country, preaching that miracles still occur, that the same Holy Spirit that causes people to speak in tongues can bring about deliverance and healing today. While many Christians were hedging a bit on how and to what degree we might expect miracles and were turning to medical science as God's venue for healing, Pentecostals were noting that Jesus himself promised we would see miracles happen (Mark 16:17; Luke 21:11, 25). The Book of James (5:14) assures us that if any are sick and call for the elders of the church and are anointed with oil, the prayer of faith will raise them up.

Dr. Westlake is among those who have witnessed miracles in the Pentecostal church: "We had a lady who had gone to a local hospital for a hysterectomy, and they found cancer wrapped around her intestines and some of her other organs. They told her that it was a very aggressive type of cancer and that she should go home because she was going to die. In spite of that advice, she kept looking for another surgeon who would do the operation; and finally she found one. She came in here on a Sunday, and my wife and I prayed for her. Then she went to the hospital on Monday. When they cut her open, they couldn't find a trace of cancer. We actually have the pathology reports from both hospitals."

Reports of such apparent miracles seem to be more common in Pentecostal circles than among others. We do regularly hear of prayers answered in our church, but we also know of many that go unanswered. The same is true in the Pentecostal church. Dr. Westlake's wife struggles with illness, though she has prayed for others and seen them healed. Yet there seems to be a greater sense of expectation within Pentecostal churches that God is, as Dr. Westlake puts it, in the "miracle-working business."

What Pentecostals Teach Us

I have mentioned that I came to know and love Christ and to have a passion for reading the Scriptures and memorizing portions of them while in a Pentecostal church. I felt a call of God on my life to be a pastor while in a Pentecostal church. I attended what was, at the time, the only officially "Charismatic" university for my undergraduate work, graduating from Oral Roberts University with a degree in pastoral ministry before going on to graduate school at Southern Methodist University. I have a great deal of appreciation for what this tradition has to offer. I also am aware of its limitations and shortcomings, which are in part why I am a United Methodist today. But there is much we have to learn from the Pentecostal faith. I was reminded of this recently while traveling.

I had flown to Arkansas to speak at a conference. As I was leaving the airport, I came upon a man who had collapsed on the floor. The paramedics were trying to resuscitate him, with no success. The police were directing everyone to move on. As I passed, I stretched out my hand toward the man to pray for him; and then I followed the directions of the police and kept moving. I had gone just a few steps when I felt a strong compulsion to go back and pray for this man and his family. It was not an audible voice, just a strong feeling. I returned to the scene, identified myself as a pastor, and asked if any members of the man's family were present. The police said that no family members were around, and again I was asked to move on. I started to leave and felt once more a strong compulsion to go back and pray for this man's family. I went back, stood at a distance, and prayed as I would have if the man had been one of my parishioners and I had been praying for him and his family at the time of death. During this time, the man passed away. After praying for a few more moments, I left the airport and went on to the conference where I was to speak. When I returned to my own church the following Sunday, I shared this story, only to learn that the man who had passed away in Arkansas was the father of one of my church members. I concluded that the Holy Spirit, knowing that my prayers for this man at his passing would be a source of comfort to his family, had compelled me to pray for him.

Some would consider this merely a coincidence. A lifetime of such experiences has led me to see them as "God-incidences," however, moments in which the Holy Spirit was leading. This is not a phenomenon unique to pastors; many people have had similar experiences. The key is to be aware and listening when the Spirit leads us.

Awareness of the presence of the Holy Spirit is one of many things we can learn from our Pentecostal friends. In particular, I want us to reflect on three strengths of Pentecostalism that we should learn from.

Living Daily in the Power and Direction of the Holy Spirit

First, Pentecostals challenge us to take seriously the role of the Holy Spirit in our lives. I graduated from a United Methodist seminary without having purchased a single book devoted to the person and work of the Holy Spirit. I had a dozen books about Jesus but only chapters within larger works about the Holy Spirit. But if the Holy Spirit truly is God's presence dwelling in our hearts, this is important news! Jesus promised that the Holy Spirit would be our counselor, our comforter, our guide. The Spirit would fill us with rivers of living water. The Spirit would convict us of sin, would give us power to be Christ's witnesses, and would help us know that we are the children of God. Clearly, we need the Holy Spirit!

While we receive the gift of the Holy Spirit's indwelling presence in our lives at the time of our baptism and salvation, this gift is like anything else God offers us. That is, God gives us the gift; then it is up to us to accept it by inviting the Spirit to work in us. I daily invite the Holy Spirit to guide me. I pray for the Spirit to fill me and use me and lead me. I pray before worship for the Holy Spirit to fill the church. I believe this is part of the reason why the congregation has grown in numbers and why people have reported so many life-changing experiences as they worshiped and became involved at the church.

Allow me to offer an analogy that might illustrate the difference in our lives made possible by a reliance on the Holy Spirit. One recent summer we had a bad windstorm, and several good-sized maple trees in my yard came down. Their thick trunks were broken off three feet above the ground; and the tops of the trees, with their dozens of branches, were lying on their sides. I needed to cut the trees off at the base, remove the branches, and then cut the trunks into pieces. I want you to imagine doing this work with a handsaw. You could do it; but it would take days, and you would be worn out. Seeing the fallen trees, my mother was kind enough to give me an early birthday present: a chainsaw! Every man's dream! Using the chainsaw, the work of cutting up the trees actually became fun and was completed in about an hour. The handsaw represents the Christian life when we have yet to invite the Holy Spirit to help. The chainsaw represents the Christian life when we invite and are open to the work and power of the Spirit. Pentecostals remind us to call on the power of the Holy Spirit so that we might experience the fullness of the Christian life.

A Willingness to Identify and Use Our Spiritual Gifts

Pentecostals have also been responsible for a renewed interest in the spiritual gifts mentioned in the Bible. While Pentecostals have often focused on the gifts that seem more exotic to the rest of us, there are a host of other spiritual gifts reported in the Scriptures, many of which we regularly see at work if only we look for them.

In 1 Corinthians 12, Paul lists gifts the Holy Spirit distributes to believers. I do not believe Paul's listing is exhaustive; it is simply illustrative. There are many other gifts. Here is the list:

> To each is given the manifestation of the Spirit for the common good. To one is given through the Spirit the utterance of wisdom, and to another the utterance of knowledge according to the same Spirit, to another faith by the same Spirit, to another gifts of healing by the one Spirit, to another the working of miracles, to another prophecy, to another the discernment of spirits, to another various kinds of tongues, to another the interpretation of tongues. All these are activated by one and the same Spirit, who allots to each one individually just as the Spirit chooses. (1 Corinthians 12:7-11)

In verse 28, Paul adds the gift of leadership/administration. In Ephesians 4:11, he adds pastors to the list of those gifted for the church. In 1 Peter 4:10-11, Peter writes that each of us should use the gifts given us to serve others; and he lists speaking and serving as two ways of doing this.

The Holy Spirit has given you certain gifts and abilities, which you likely were born with. You may have been equipped with other gifts since becoming a Christian. God's expectation is that you use those gifts to serve others, to build up the body of Christ, to further his work, and to glorify him.

One Friday night recently our contemporary choir was performing. I was standing in the back of the sanctuary when Bruce, one of our trustees, said, "Isn't it amazing to see the various gifts people have and how they use them here?" He was right. It is awesome. Then he said, "If I got up there to sing, they'd be paying to get out of here!" I do not know about Bruce's vocal talents, but I do know that he has administrative and leadership talents that have been invaluable to our church. Bruce's gifts allow those who sing to use their gifts for God's glory and the edification of the church. Those who have gifts of compassion use their gifts in mercy ministries, and those who have teaching gifts use those gifts in helping others. When we use our gifts—God's gifts given to us for his purposes—we find joy in our faith.

If you are interested in discovering your spiritual gifts, talk with your pastor or some other leader in your church. Or just try serving in some area of the church and see how it works. The key is that you have been given a gift, and you are meant to use it![2]

Reclaiming Healing Power

Finally, our Pentecostal friends challenge us to be bold in praying and to expect that God can do wonderful things to heal our bodies. We are often timid about this, and I understand some of the reasons. We know God does not always miraculously intervene. In fact, we know God's ordinary way of working is through our bodies' healing mechanisms and through physicians and medicine. But prayer does accomplish great good and plays a role in healing.

I believe in and have witnessed miracles from time to time. I always invite God to work to bring complete healing to those who are sick. I encourage patients and their families to rely on doctors and nurses and medication, but also on friends who care for them and the witness of the Spirit that can comfort all of us. I have seen people who I was certain would die, live. And I have been with people whom thousands were praying for who, nevertheless, died. But I am certain that one way or another, God heard and answered each of those prayers.

All of which leads me to summarize this chapter on Pentecostalism by encouraging you to invite the Holy Spirit to be at work in your life. This does not necessarily require speaking in tongues or exotic expressions of power. But it will result in your experiencing and being more aware of the Spirit's guidance, power, and work in your life. Let me encourage you to offer this simple prayer on a regular basis:

> Come, Holy Spirit, and fill me anew. Guide me. Use me. Empower me. Lead me. Grant me your gifts that I might be useful to you in serving others. In Jesus' name. Amen.

1. See www.regent.edu/news/lectures_azusastreet.html
2. You might also be interested in a resource written by two persons in the church I serve as pastor. This eight-week study, entitled *Serving From the Heart* (Abingdon Press, 2002), can help you discover your spiritual gifts.

CHAPTER 8

METHODISM:
PEOPLE OF THE EXTREME CENTER

When he left there, he met Jehonadab son of Rechab com-
ing to meet him; he greeted him, and said to him, "Is your
heart as true to mine as mine is to yours?" Jehonadab
answered, "It is." Jehu said, "If it is, give me your hand."

(2 Kings 10:15)

When the Pharisees heard that he had silenced the
Sadducees, they gathered together, and one of them, a lawyer,
asked him a question to test him. "Teacher, which command-
ment in the law is the greatest?" He said to him, " 'You shall
love the Lord your God with all your heart, and with all your
soul, and with all your mind.' This is the greatest and first com-
mandment."

(Matthew 22:34-38)

A Brief History of Methodism

Methodism was born out of the struggle of ideas that took place in England from the sixteenth century to the beginning of the eighteenth century. The conflict between Roman Catholicism and Protestantism in England had led to bloodshed and even civil war as England's monarchs severed ties to Rome, reestablished them, then severed and reestablished them again. Ultimately, England's church would be Protestant; but the question became, "How Protestant?" The struggle for control of the Church of England was a three-way tug of war among Roman Catholics, more-radical Protestant reformers (Puritans who wanted to purify or purge the English church of Catholic influence), and those who sought a middle way between these two. As we have seen, it was the middle way (the *via media*) that ultimately prevailed, but not without tremendous religious turmoil and protest.

We might picture this period of England's history as the swinging of a pendulum between religious ideas. After two hundred years of turmoil among the three groups described above, a new movement called the Enlightenment offered those frustrated with the old religious debates salvation through knowledge and reason. People ascribing to Enlightenment principles retained membership in the church and formally held that they were Christians, but increasingly their allegiance to Christianity was in name only. Partly as a result of this trend, religious vitality and morals declined during the eighteenth century; and this produced another reaction—another swing of the pendulum—known as Pietism. Among the impulses of the Pietists was the formation of religious "societies" or groups aimed at fostering holiness. These groups often taught that reason was deceptive and that truth was found in the heart and in the spiritual realm, not in the realm of reason.

Knowing something about all these forces is helpful in understanding Methodists because in profound ways Methodism was shaped by them and by their impact on one man: John Wesley.

Introducing John Wesley

John Wesley, born June 17, 1703, was the fifteenth of nineteen children of Samuel and Susanna Wesley, nine of whom died in infancy. Wesley's grandfathers had been "Dissenters," also referred to as "Nonconformists" (terms used to describe those who were dissatisfied with the official state church and who formed their own churches). Wesley's parents, however, were a part of the established church, his father being a priest in the Church of England. Thus, even in Wesley's own family the tensions and challenges of theological debates were present.

John ultimately followed his father's footsteps into the ministry, studying at Christ Church (College), Oxford. There young John felt a desire for God and for a more-rigorous faith than he saw among many of his classmates. In 1725, he wrote that his desire was no longer to be a "nominal" Christian but to be a "real" Christian. Following his ordination and a brief stint in the local church, he returned to Oxford, where he began to meet with a group of college students who also longed for a more-rigorous faith. These students worshiped together and pursued acts of charity in the community. Their methodical approach to the pursuit of holiness earned them the name "Methodist" among their critics. The name stuck.

Wesley was shaped both by the spirit of the Enlightenment and by the Pietist movement that was skeptical of reason, holding these seemingly opposing forces together in tension with each other. This union of reason with the desire for a personal faith would become a defining characteristic of Methodism. To this day United Methodists see themselves as people who bring together both a reasonable faith that is intellectually satisfying and a passionate and emotionally compelling faith that touches the heart.

In the early years, Wesley's own faith leaned more toward the intellect, though he had a deep yearning to experience an assurance of salvation. At the age of thirty-five, after a failed mission to America, Wesley became increasingly aware of his own lack of faith. Then, in 1738, Wesley had what he considered to be a profound conversion experience. As he listened to the words of Martin Luther being read—words reflecting upon the teaching of justification by faith—he reported, "I felt my heart strangely warmed. I felt I did trust in Christ, Christ alone for salvation; and an assurance was given me that He had taken away my sins, even mine, and saved me from the law of sin and death."[1]

Wesley had known a faith of the intellect, but now he knew a faith of the warm heart as well. He demonstrated a new passion and religious zeal following this experience. His passion was at times denounced by his colleagues as "enthusiasm," a term of derision in the eighteenth century. Yet his ability to hold together reason and a passionate faith has led many to describe him, and early Methodists, as "reasonable enthusiasts."

When Wesley's friend George Whitefield asked him to come and preach in the fields, a practice that Wesley initially viewed as improper and distasteful, he declined. In April of 1739, however, he finally relented and agreed to preach outdoors. Wesley wrote in his journal, "On Monday at four in the afternoon, I submitted to 'be more vile' and proclaimed in the highways the glad tidings of salvation, speaking from a little mound in a ground adjoining the city to about three thousand people!"[2] There was no turning back from this form of preaching. Wesley proclaimed that the "world is my parish." He would spend the rest of his life preaching in the open air, and in churches when invited. It is said that he rode over 250,000 miles by horseback traversing the British Isles, preaching and calling people to follow Jesus Christ.

In this sense Wesley shares similarities with the twentieth-century evangelist Billy Graham, whose outdoor revivals led millions to make a decision to follow Christ. By the time of Wesley's death, he was a national hero; and his preaching and leadership had changed the course of history.

If we were to show how United Methodists see our chart of church history, we would find that Methodism emerged from the Anglican Church in the eighteenth century, seeking to provide a middle way between the Church of England and the more-puritanical movements that became the Baptist and Congregational churches. The chart, as seen by Methodists, would look something like this:

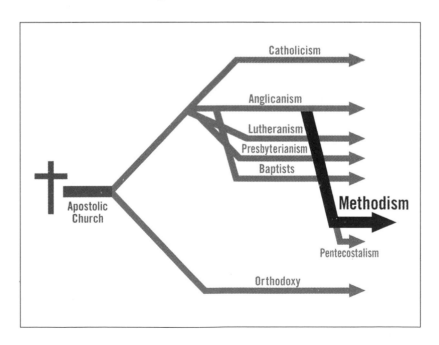

Early Methodists

Methodism began as a renewal movement within the Church of England. Wesley had no intention of starting a new church. An Anglican priest, no doubt influenced by his dissenting grandparents and clearly influenced by the Pietism of his day, he believed the Church of England was in need of reformation; and he wanted his ministry to help revitalize it. To that end he not only preached but also published books. Wesley also organized those who had been touched by his preaching. He invited those who had made a commitment to Christ to join the movement through the United Societies. ("Societies" were religious groups that encouraged members in their pursuit of God and Christian mission. There were many of these societies in the eighteenth century, and several are still active in England today.) Members were called to live by three simple rules, known by members of the Methodist societies as the "General Rules." Methodists were required to:

1. Avoid doing what you know is wrong.
2. Do all the good you can to everyone that you can.
3. Pursue the spiritual disciplines, including prayer, worship, Scripture reading, and fasting, among others.

United Methodist pastors are still charged, at ordination, with upholding these General Rules.

Three practices shaped the Methodist movement and continue to shape United Methodism to this day. The first was preaching. Wesley knew that in preaching, people came to faith, heard God's will, and had their lives changed. He preached thousands of times; and those who became Methodists and had the gift for speaking—both clergy and a large number of laypeople—began following in his footsteps, preaching in the open fields and calling people to faith. Methodists became known for outstanding preaching.

Second, Wesley organized those who had repented of their sin and sought to live for Christ into small groups so that they could hold one another accountable and help one another grow in grace. In the contemporary church, the small-group movement has been very important. In some ways this is the reclaiming of a practice made popular by the eighteenth-century Methodists.

Finally, the Methodists were known for their singing. Wesley's brother Charles was a prolific hymn writer, penning what was, at the time, "contemporary" music that captured the theology and practices of the Methodists. He wrote thousands of hymns, many of which are still sung today, including "O For a Thousand Tongues to Sing"; "Hark! The Herald Angels Sing"; "Christ the Lord Is Risen Today"; and "Love Divine, All Loves Excelling," to name just a few.

In addition to their fervor in calling people to conversion, Methodists were also social reformers. Wesley believed Jesus called his followers to be involved in the transformation of society. Wesley organized a school for children, raised funds for the poor, spoke out against slavery and other social ills of his time, visited the prisons, and called for prison reform. He did not see the concern for transforming society, or the "social gospel" as it would later be called, as being at odds with the evangelical gospel or the invitation for people to put their trust in Christ. He saw these as two dimensions of the same gospel.

Beliefs and Practices of Methodism

Let's consider some of the characteristic beliefs and practices of Methodism and some of the forces that shaped John Wesley and, in turn, the Methodist movement.

United Methodists, along with nearly all the denominations and families of Christianity we have studied in this book, accept the Nicene Creed and Apostles' Creed as containing the core tenets of the Christian faith; and many United Methodist congregations recite one or the other weekly in their worship services. Affirming the Apostles' Creed is a part of the baptismal liturgy of The United Methodist Church to the present day. While the creeds appear in *The United Methodist Hymnal* and *The Book of Worship,* the officially binding theological statements are not the creeds, but what are called the "Articles of Religion," which affirm, in one way or another, the faith statements given in the creeds. These articles are drawn from the Anglican Church's Articles of Religion but are reduced in number from thirty-nine to twenty-five. In addition to these basic affirmations of the Christian faith, I would mention seven characteristics of Methodism:

*Wesley and subsequent generations of Methodists were **ecumenical** and willing to work with and learn from Christians of other denominations.* The very idea of a book like the one you are holding in your hands, one that focuses on growing as Christians by listening to others, is in many ways characteristic of Methodists. As we have noted, Wesley and his generation inherited 200 years of religious warfare. Even in his own home he had experienced religious debates. Perhaps partly as a result of these debates, Wesley was led to look for common ground and to build bridges with people who thought differently than he did. In one of Wesley's most-famous printed sermons, "Catholic Spirit," he wrote, "Although a difference in opinions or modes of worship may prevent an entire external union, yet need it prevent our union in affection? Though we can't think alike, may we not love alike? May we not be of one heart, though we are not of one opinion? Without all doubt we may. Herein all the children of God may unite, notwithstanding these smaller differences."[3]

These words are still refreshing 250 years after Wesley first penned them, and they capture part of the spirit of Methodism. United Methodists tend to build bridges with other Christians rather than erect walls that separate.

*Methodists believe in bringing their **intellect** to their faith.* Although Wesley set aside that strain of the Enlightenment that had rejected faith and experience, he is often seen as a child of the Enlightenment in his embrace of reason and intellect as valid (though imperfect) ways of pursuing God. Wesley's impulse, captured in a phrase variously attributed to either John or Charles Wesley, was always to "unite the two so long divided—knowledge and vital piety." Wesley was a voracious reader and writer who embraced the intellect as a gift from God. United Methodists still value the intellect and believe they are not to "check their brain at the door" when they enter the church.

*Wesley and the early Methodists valued **passion** and **experience**.* It was Wesley's own experience of assurance that propelled and empowered him in his ministry. He embraced experience as a means of knowing God, though he himself was critical of the emotional excess that was sometimes seen in the Methodist movement. This combination of reason and experience, of the intellectual pursuit of God with spiritual fervor and passion, is part of the basic makeup of Methodism. Wesley considered experience such an important part of faith that he added it to the Anglicans' three-legged stool of Scripture, tradition, and reason to create what we refer to today as the Wesleyan quadrilateral.

One of my favorite movies is the 1992 film *A River Runs Through It,* based on the book by Norman Maclean. Maclean tells the story of his father, a Scot and a Presbyterian pastor in the early twentieth century. In the movie Maclean's father refers to Methodists of that time as "Baptists who can read." The phrase was meant as an insult to both Baptists and Methodists, but I believe it contained a grain of truth; namely, that Methodists possess the passion and evangelical fervor of the Baptists, coupled with a passion for the intellect and the pursuit of knowledge.

*Wesley and the Methodists, drawing from the Pietist movement, placed major emphasis on a **personal faith**.* Wesley was specifically influenced by German Pietism, a reform movement within Lutheranism that began in the seventeenth century. Pietism emphasized the need for the "new birth" and stressed the importance of the spiritual disciplines, the personal devotional life, the laity in the church, and small-group meetings to study the Scriptures. Wesley embraced all these emphases and incorporated them into the Methodist movement, and they are still an important part of United Methodism today.

Wesley and the Methodists stood against Calvin's teaching on predestination. Wesley vigorously argued that God has not predestined some to everlasting life and others to hell, insisting that God's grace is available to and working in all of us and that we are free to accept it or reject it. Today, United Methodists continue to place a strong emphasis on **free will** and reject the idea of predestination. They accept the idea that God may know in advance what will happen and who will choose God, but they reject the idea that God has foreordained who will inherit eternal life.

Wesley brought together the **high-church** *tradition of the Anglicans with the* **low-church** *simplicity of worship that characterized Puritan churches.* Wesley valued the traditions of the church; but he also seemed to share his grandparents' Puritan tendencies, arguing for simplicity in worship and life. While Puritans stripped their churches of altars, Wesley retained them; while Anglicans held to a very liturgical form of worship, Wesley allowed a freer and less-formal service. In most United Methodist services today, we find elements of worship that are Anglican, although less liturgical, along with elements of the Presbyterian worship that sprang from the Puritan traditions.

Wesley placed major emphasis on two seemingly contradictory ideas: **grace** *and* **holiness***.* Methodists recognize that it is only by God's grace (God's undeserved favor and blessings) that we have life and salvation. Our salvation is purely a gift from God. Methodists tend to emphasize, with the psalmists, that God is "merciful and gracious, / slow to anger and abounding in steadfast love" (Psalm 86:15; 103:8). At the same time, Methodists believe that we are saved from sin in order to do good works. Wesley emphasized a doctrine called sanctification, or what was also referred to as Christian perfection or simply holiness, championing this ideal as the lifelong goal of the believer. Sanctification or holiness means to have one's heart so transformed by the power of the Holy Spirit that one manifests perfect love for God and neighbor. Wesley believed that it was possible to be wholly sanctified in this life and that, by the pursuit of God and the yielding of one's life to the work of the Holy Spirit, anyone might receive from God this gift of sanctification.

Holiness, for Methodists, has two dimensions: the love of God, which means surrendering completely to God while avoiding anything that would offend God in one's thoughts, words, and deeds, and the love of neighbor, which includes caring for the poor, the sick, and those in need, thereby addressing injustice and seeking to shape our communities so that they are patterned on the kingdom of God. These twin dimensions of holiness are sometimes referred to as personal holiness and social holiness.

What I value most about Methodism is its attempt at holding together so many seemingly disparate ideas and practices: the emphasis on both the social and evangelical gospels; the linking of God's grace with a call to holiness and good works; the coupling of personal, passionate experience with a serious intellect; the love of both liturgy and simplicity in worship; and Wesley's firm belief that God is sovereign and yet has given human beings free will, inviting all to receive God's grace. These beliefs are not necessarily unique to Methodists; many of the families of faith we have studied share them. But for United Methodists these polarities tend to be one of the defining characteristics of their faith.

I asked Bishop Scott Jones of the Kansas Area of The United Methodist Church to describe Methodism. Here is his reply:

In the Christian faith, there are people who are extreme right and people who are extreme left. But whether it's clergy clothing or how our services of worship are conducted or how we read the Bible, we tend to be people of the extreme center. The extreme center means that The United Methodist Church at its best is conservative in some areas and liberal in other areas. We don't fit a stereotype very well. For example, some denominations are good at helping nominally religious and nonreligious people enter into the Christian life. Well, that's part of the gospel; and it's part of what we do as United Methodists. Other denominations want to help the poor and address social issues, however they define them. Well, that's part of the gospel; and Methodists embrace that as well. The center is a very hard position to maintain because there are always people who are sniping at you from the extremes. Sometimes it's easier to hold an extreme position because you can be really clear and really forceful, but what you are lacking is the perspective of your brothers and sisters who disagree with you. By occupying the extreme center, we see the value of both sides and try to carve out a position, whether it involves theology or social justice, that embraces the whole gospel.

John Wesley's Passions

I want to wrap up our look at Methodism by mentioning three of Wesley's passions, things he devoted his life to doing. The first was to **change lives**. He wanted to find people who did not know Christ—nonreligious and nominally religious people—and invite them to become followers of the Savior. He wanted to see lives changed.

The second passion of John Wesley was to **transform the world**. He believed in spreading "Scriptural holiness across the land," which included helping shape society to look like the kingdom of God. This passion could be seen in the early Methodists' ministry to the poor and their willingness to speak to the social issues of their time.

Wesley's third passion was to **revitalize the church**. He did not intend to start a new denomination but rather to reinvigorate and reform the Church of England in his day.

The church I serve as pastor has sought to capture these three ideas in our vision statement. Our vision is to reach people whom other churches are not reaching, helping them become deeply committed Christians; to transform our community so that it looks more like the kingdom of God; and to be a catalyst for renewal within our denomination and mainline Christianity. These same impulses inspired John Wesley and the early Methodists.

United Methodists invite other Christians to listen to and learn from one another; to recognize that truth is often found most fully not on the extremes, but in the center; and to pursue the life of faith by maintaining a balance between grace and holiness, intellect and emotion, evangelism and social justice.

1. From *The Works of John Wesley,* edited by Albert C. Outler (Abingdon Press, 1988); Vol. 18; entry for May 24, 1738.

2. From *The Works of John Wesley,* edited by Albert C. Outler (Abingdon Press, 1990); Vol. 19; entry for April 2, 1739.

3. From "Catholic Spirit," by John Wesley, in *The Works of John Wesley,* edited by Albert C. Outler (Abingdon Press, 1985); Vol 2.

CHRISTIANITY'S FAMILY TREE

I began this book by telling you about my family reunion. Family members from across the country came to the event, and it was a delight to be there. As we gathered, I found that there were some people I did not recognize at all, as well as others I had known all my life. I walked to the food line and dished up my barbeque, and then I went to sit down for lunch. And where did I sit? Not with the people who had traveled across the country, but with the brothers and sisters I see all the time! Why did I sit there? Because it was my comfort zone. I knew them best. After a few minutes it struck me: "I can talk with my brothers and sisters anytime. I really need to get to know these other family members."

So I took my barbeque and began going from table to table, just sitting down and talking with my family. There was my cousin David from Boulder, who was a hippie in the 1970s and is still a bit of a hippie even now. There was his straight-laced brother D. J., a successful businessman in Dallas. There was "Larry Boy" from Arkansas, who can fix anything. And David and D. J. and Larry Boy's children and grandchildren were all in the room. I could see that these cousins passed on their differences to their children.

As the reunion came to an end, I was still trying to remember exactly how each of these persons was related to me. Then I remembered: My great-grandmother Richardson was the mother, grandmother, great-grandmother, or great-great-grandmother of every single person in that room. We all were connected by a single person. The same thing is true of the Christian family. We all are connected through a person: Jesus Christ.

In this book I have just skimmed the surface of the beliefs and practices of eight groups in Christianity's family tree. Some members of these groups would likely disagree with my summaries or would add or take away this or that idea. I hope none of my descriptions is too far afield. My aim in writing this book has been to help you gain an appreciation for the richness of the various Christian traditions, to understand a bit of church history, and to look for ways in which your own Christian experience might be enriched by exploring the faith and practices of others in the Christian family.

Let's look once again at the complete chart of all the churches we have studied, shown on the facing page.

There are the two main branches—Orthodox (Eastern) and Catholic (Western)—with the final division occurring in AD 1054. We have the Lutherans, who began the Protestant Reformation of the Western church, followed by Calvin and the Reformed churches, most notably the Presbyterians. We find the Anglicans, who, under Henry VIII, formally left the Roman Catholic Church in 1534. We see the Baptists, who sprang from the Puritan renewal movement within the Church of England in the 1600s, as well as the United Methodists, who began in the 1700s as a renewal movement in the Church of England. Finally we have the Pentecostals, who trace their history back through the Methodist movement. Each of these lines represents a part of the family of

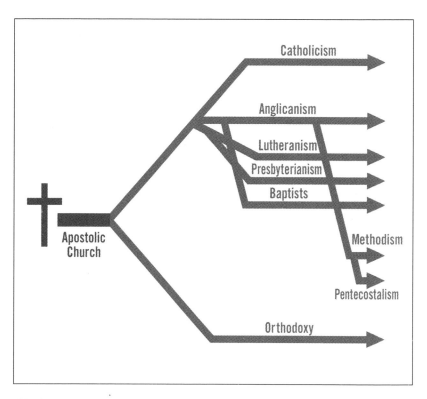

Christ that thought it needed to correct the shortcomings of the others or that sought to reform the church. Each group thought it was doing the right thing and had the clearest picture of the gospel.

Some of you may note that your denomination is not one of the eight we have studied. Of course, there are thousands of Christian groups. It would be impossible to study them all in this book. However, as you study your own denominational heritage, I believe you will find your tradition emerging from one or more of the traditions we have studied in this book.

Although we were not able to include all the additional denominations in this book, we can add some to our chart, which might change it to look something like this:

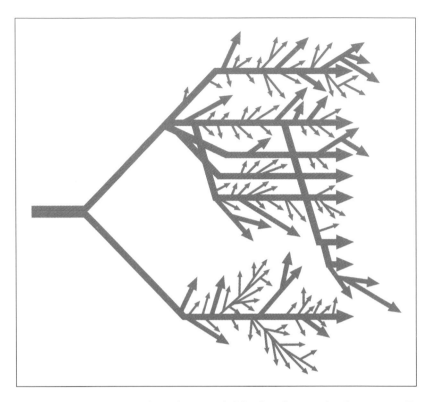

As you can see, the chart quickly begins to look messy. It represents many different denominations. Yet even this augmented chart portrays only a fraction of the denominations in existence, each of which believes that it has a clearer picture of the gospel or that its practices are more faithful than those of the rest.

As I pondered this chart, something occurred to me. I began to wonder, What would happen if the chart were turned on end?

And that is when I saw it. Maybe the best image of the church is not so much a chart, showing hundreds or even thousands of denominations offering competing truths, each thinking it is the true church; instead, maybe the reality is that all these churches together are like a tree.

When we view the body of Christ as a tree, there are several things we begin to realize. Wouldn't it be unhealthy if we tried to cut off all the other branches, leaving only our own branch? Or, how absurd to think of one branch saying, "We are the whole tree." How tragic would that be? The beauty of the tree—its glory—comes from its many different branches.

Gazing at the tree, we are reminded that all the branches share the same roots and trunk. Our roots are Judaism. Our trunk is Jesus Christ. Permeating the entire tree is the Holy Spirit, which feeds the leaves and allows the tree to grow. When we look at the church in this way, I am moved to say,

"How beautiful is the body of Christ! How grateful I am for all its branches!"

This is how I believe it really is with God and the church. This realization about Christianity's family tree makes me grateful for my brothers and sisters who are Orthodox, Catholic, Lutheran, Presbyterian, Episcopalian, Baptist, Pentecostal, and United Methodist, as well as for all the rest we did not specifically consider in this book. We may disagree with one another on this or that issue. We may feel more comfortable in this church or that. But we all are nourished by the same sap, connected to the same trunk, anchored by the same roots. Together we are the body of Christ. As we conclude this study, I invite you to make this your prayer:

Lord, thank you for your church. Each branch has a beauty all its own. Forgive us for the times when we have looked down on your other children. Forgive us for secretly believing we are your favorites. Help us to learn from our brothers and sisters of other Christian denominations. Help us to love one another. And help us to work together, that we might accomplish your purposes for your church. Bless our friends of other denominations, as well as those who are part of nondenominational churches. Help us in humility and love to bless them all and to see them as your beloved children. Amen.

FOR FURTHER READING

Frank S. Mead, Samuel S. Hill, and Craig D. Atwood, *Handbook of Denominations in the United States,* 12th Edition. Nashville: Abingdon Press, 2005.
A classic survey of denominational families and groups that is updated periodically, this book offers some of the most up-to-date information about the history and current state of denominations large and small in the United States.

Catherine L. Albanese, *America: Religion and Religions.* Belmont, California: Wadsworth Publishing, 2006.
A basic introduction to American religious history, this volume sets the denominations in the larger context of culture, ethnicity, controversy, and their identity in the United States.

Carter Lindberg, *A Brief History of Christianity.* Boston: Blackwell Publishing, 2005.
This book offers the broader context for the development of Catholicism and Protestantism and their basic beliefs and practices. An excellent introduction to general studies.

Martin E. Marty, *Pilgrims in Their Own Land: 500 Years of Religion in America.* New York: Penguin, 1985.
This volume provides invaluable historical and anecdotal information regarding developments in American religious history. Names, dates, and movements are punctuated by superb historical vignettes that enliven the study.

Chester Gillis, *Roman Catholicism in America.* New York: Columbia University Press, 2000.
One volume in a series of studies on American religious groups published by Columbia University Press, this work explores the nature of Catholicism as it developed in the United States from the early missionaries, to the nineteenth-century immigrants, through Vatican II and the election of John F. Kennedy (the nation's first Catholic president). A valuable resource for understanding the Catholic ethos in America.

Bill J. Leonard, *Baptists in America.* New York: Columbia University Press, 2005.
Another volume in the Columbia University Press series, this book traces the history of the Baptists with particular attention to the multiplicity of "Baptist ways" of doing church; their many controversies; and current debates over ordination of women, sexuality, religious liberty, and biblical authority.

Sean Michael Lucas, *On Being Presbyterian: Our Beliefs, Practices, and Stories.* Phillipsburg, NJ: P & R Publishing, 2006.
This basic introduction to Presbyterian history and practice is a well-written survey text with good information.

David Hein and Gardiner H. Shattuck, Jr., *The Episcopalians.* New York: Church Publishing, 2005.
This basic introduction to Episcopalian/Anglican history and beliefs is a good survey of beliefs and practices.

Kristofer Skrade and James Satter, *The Lutheran Handbook.* Minneapolis: Augsburg Fortress, 2005.
This is a basic introduction to Lutheran beliefs, creeds, and polity.

James E. Kirby, Russell E. Richey, and Kenneth E. Rowe, *The Methodists: Student Edition.* Westport, Connecticut: Praeger, 1998.
This popular approach to Methodist history and polity is a well-written survey.